FOREWORD

by

Bridgett Walther, author

Valerie Beth Gilbert is one of a kind. Well, of course she is: a sassy Greek New Yorker who knows the city and subway system better than anyone else I know. Full disclosure: I LOVE and RESPECT Valerie and her work. I love publishing her wry, witty, sometimes gut-wrenching, and always TRUE stories on my front page. If you want to know what New York is about from a guide with a brilliant sense of it and its history, and all with a wild sense of humor, *talk to Valerie*. She knows the best pizza joints, coffee shops, and one-of-kind gourmet restaurants. That's where we go to celebrate good times together! She lives and breathes the city. Valerie is also a gifted guide for truly magical, healing meditations. She's Ms. New York, and my virtual sister. Damn, I'm so proud of her! You will treasure this book, re-read it repeatedly, and tell your friends to buy it. Yeah. She's THAT good! - Bridgett Walther, author, *Conquer the Cosmos*, (Penguin/Plume) and owner, http://www.bridgettwalther.com.

Astrologers Bridgett Walther and Hazel Dixon-Cooper (represented by Dupree-Miller & Associates) are writing a book about Pluto, to be published by Beyond Words in early 2014.

Dead mothers, missing husbands, disgusting dates, perverted "reverends," seductive gurus, infamous ingrates, and cheese thieves. These are just a few of the cast of characters that pepper Valerie Gilbert's true tales in *Raving Violet*.

Enter the world of a solitary but intrepid New Yorker. Orphaned as a young adult, this divorced, smartass metaphysician has sought solace and insight from philosophers, séances, channels and mediums—a path that has, inevitably, led her back to her formidable fortress within.

Join Valerie as she scales the castle walls on her journey for love, sex, sass, a chuckle, and really good chocolate. Love and Loss! Love and Glory! Love and Nausea! *Raving Violet* has it all.

KUDOS for *Raving Violet*

Who but Valerie Gilbert, the razor-witted, New York-bred, Harvard-educated author of Raving Violet, could claim "I may be crazy but I'm not stupid" while weaving achingly poignant tales of boundless spiritual optimism into tapestries of mysticism, inimitable opinion and hope. Love, loss, skepticism and belief are featured threads liberally doused with a double shot of comedic hilarity in this luminous compilation of observational essays. Part brainiac's diary, part comedic actress's stand-up routine, Raving Violet brilliantly showcases this provocateur's unwavering search for life's enchantment while equally willing to riff on its ridiculousness. Where some writers have a way with words, Ms. Gilbert has a way with whole phrases that leave you wishing you had a best friend like her to stand by you at the loom of life. – *Andrea Chait, Blogger, "Girl Out of the City," England*

A must read for those seeking to change their lives for the better, to shed negative energy and empower themselves. Valerie Gilbert's voice is thought provoking with a perfect balance of wisdom, humor and inspiration. – *Debbie Christiana, author of Twin Flames and Solstice* (to be released mid-2013)

RAVING VIOLET

By

VALERIE GILBERT

A Black Opal Books Publication

GENRE: NON-FICTION/HUMOR/MEMOIRS

This book is a work of non-fiction. All information and opinions expressed herein are the views of the author. This publication is for informational purposes only. Neither the author nor the publisher is attempting to provide legal advice of any kind. All trademarks, service marks, registered trademarks, and registered service marks are the property of their respective owners and are used herein for identification purposes only. Some names may have been changed at the author's discretion or at the request of the person or persons involved. The publisher does not have any control over or assume any responsibility for author or third-party websites or their contents.

RAVING VIOLET
© 2013 by Valerie Gilbert
All Rights Reserved
Cover Design by Jackson Cover Designs
© 2013 All Rights Reserved
Print ISBN: 978-1-937329-84-6

First publication: JANUARY 2013

All rights reserved under the International and Pan-American Copyright Conventions. No part of this book may be reproduced or transmitted in any form or by any means, electronic or mechanical, including photocopying, recording, or by any information storage and retrieval system, without permission in writing from the publisher.

WARNING: The unauthorized reproduction or distribution of this copyrighted work is illegal. Criminal copyright infringement, including infringement without monetary gain, is investigated by the FBI and is punishable by up to 5 years in federal prison and a fine of $250,000.

ABOUT THE PRINT VERSION: If you purchased a print version of this book without a cover, you should be aware that the book is stolen property. It was reported as "unsold and destroyed" to the publisher, and neither the author nor the publisher has received any payment for this "stripped book."

IF YOU FIND A PRINT VERSION OF THIS BOOK BEING SOLD OR SHARED ILLEGALLY, PLEASE REPORT IT TO OUR LEGAL DEPARTMENT AT: lpn@blackopalbooks.com.

Published by Black Opal Books: **http://www.blackopalbooks.com**

DEDICATION

Dedicated to: Bridgett Walther, my Sexy Fairy Godmother and most stunning and steadfast cheerleader, without whom this book would not exist. She is mentor, souful sister, and fiercely loyal champion all in one.

To my parents, without whom *I* would not exist, and whose longtime residence in "the beyond" has inspired me to learn more about where, exactly, they live.

And (surprise!) to ME, since I AM fan-fucking-tastic. I'm all about self-love. You'll see.

I would like to thank those who sustained me when I was lower than low from the time my mom got sick when I was in college: heartfelt shout outs to Ellen Haley, wherever she is, who gave me biofeedback therapy at University Health Services. She introduced me to Brian Eno's "Music for Airports" song 1/1 which has been calming me down since 1983. To Mark Ganem, writer, editor, restaurateur and friend extraordinaire, for encouraging me to write, and Diane Burkam for actually paying for one of my writing classes and numerous psychic sessions. To David Arias for being so gosh darn loyal. To Bill Coyle for being himself, which means funny, insightful, and human. To my cousin Genia, who has always been there with her ever so generous heart.

To my stalwart and loving friends Andrea, Laura, Kristen, Carey and Marisa - friends like family. To my dear neighbors Frank and Michelle, who sustained me (and my pets) while I underwent and recovered from surgery.

A special thank you to my dear friend Sister Eileen O'Keefe, a kindred spirit who shares my heart and birthday. Thank you, Eileen, for your sincere kindness, impish support, generosity and enthusiasm over the years.

Thanks always to my spirit teachers. Milarepa, Orkie, Hieronymous, and Paul Selig's "Guides", whoever they are. To whomever supports me energetically when I write, and to my guides and teachers in spirit generally. We all have an entourage. Plug in!

Last but not least, to my new friends at Black Opal Books. With deepest gratitude to Lauri Wellington for selecting me for the Grand Prize, an entrée into the world of published authors. I am eternally grateful to Lauri, L.P. and Mike for believing in me. I believe in them! They are the magic that makes the Black Opal glow. With gratitude to Black Opal Editors Lauri, Faith and Susan, and to Jack for the super gorgeous cover art he envisioned and brought to life. What a gift the Black Opal experience has been.

Table of Contents

Introduction..1

Chapter 1:
Don't Have Any Fun!..5

Chapter 2:
Label Me Dumb..9

Chapter 3:
Stacking The Deck..15

Chapter 4:
Bees Wax..22

Chapter 5:
Finding Gardens...29

Chapter 6:
The Buck Stops Here..35

Chapter 7:
Rock…Paper…Scissors..43

Chapter 8:
Batman and Jose...51

Chapter 9:
Fuck The Post...59

Chapter 10:
The Law of Bananas...70

Chapter 11:
What A Real Man Does...79

Chapter 12:
The Gerry Bear..86

Chapter 13:
A Tale Of Two Soldiers..98

Chapter 14:
The Woman With Bubbles On Her Knee......................108

Chapter 15:
"So You Think You Can Dance, Jesus and Mary?"..........118

Chapter 16:
The Gypsy Curse…A Cautionary Tale............................129

Chapter 17:
Satyha Sigh…Baba Au Rhum..140

Chapter 18:
Peter, Paul and Me-Ary (I mean me)..............................150

Chapter 19:
The Cheese Thief (A Scary Story)...................................164

Chapter 20:
How Many Glasses of Wine?...182

Chapter 21:
Love Like The Sun..195

Chapter 22:
I Remember Mama..214

Chapter 23:
Chatting With The Dead...226

INTRODUCTION

Embarrassing! Terrible! Bad! That's what I thought as I started to review for this book the essays that began as my brand new blog back in September of 2011. It depressed me to read them. Maybe *all* my short stories were terrible, I'd just been deluding myself that they were good. Maybe *I* just sucked, generally? But as I continued to read, review, and edit the pieces, I realized just how powerful and necessary each one was to my process. I couldn't have gotten to the third piece ("Stacking the Deck," where I really start to find my voice) if I hadn't written the first two.

Looking back on my first essay in September of 2011, unsure of where I was going, I decided to dive in by commenting on a piece I read in a local NYC paper I found on the bus. My first few chapters were rants (hence "Raving" Violet). As I started to review them for this book, I felt uncomfortable, but I don't think they're terrible anymore, in fact, I think they're terrific. They represent the genesis of my voice. Follow the Yellow Brick Road. How do you get there from here? It often seems a daunting, insurmountable, undoable task, especially if you don't know where you're going.

Two quotes come to mind. One, from a poster I bought as a youngster at sleepaway music camp in Michigan: "If you don't know where you're going, you'll probably end up somewhere else." And from J.R.R. Tolkein: "All who wander are not lost." Contradictory, aren't they? I love them both. Confusion is a *terrific* state of mind to be in. It means you're no longer stuck in the rut of thinking you know everything. You're off-kilter, uncertain, and ready to carve new neural pathways in your brain if you keep pushing forward instead of reverting to old default modes. Confusion is a sign that great, imminent change is possible.

Could Dorothy have even contemplated the existence of Emerald City when she wandered the dusty roads of Kansas with her dog? Of course not. All she knew was that she had to leave what was known, but no longer safe, behind.

This is what *I've* learned. Bloom where you're planted. Put one foot in front of the other. Start somewhere, ANYWHERE. But start. Go. Write. Be. Speak. Tap dance. Take that cooking class, learn Tuvan throat singing. Whatever it is you're curious about, heed Lao Tzu, "A journey of a thousand miles begins with a single step." Take it. Create your path. Find your voice. Be daring. Be brave.

You'll never do it if you judge and criticize everything you do and let fear freeze you in place. Trust the flow of life, the flow of your voice, your footsteps, and you will be flying joyously without a net before long. Now, get going!

CHAPTER 1

DON'T HAVE ANY FUN!

September 26, 2011

That's right, you heard me right, I said, "Do not have any fun." That's what the government wants you to do, or rather, the "rogue" element within our government, and the "Corporatocracy" that controls our G-men. I just walked by another gang of SWAT guys (and one tiny gal) all gussied up for serious combat on the corner of 42nd Street and Third Avenue. It was Sunday, September 25, 2011. What was the occasion? I don't bother asking anymore, I just smile my love at them.

The last time I inquired as to why a small, heavily armed gang was on the corner of 57th Street and Third Avenue (perhaps protecting the Duane Reade drug store?) I got the generic response "Protecting the country, ma'am!" or something to that effect. I laughed and said, "Well, I sure feel safe! Carry on!" It amuses me no end that these soldiers are planted here to remind us of the fact that we are, according to them, "not safe." I for one, am safe. I claim it, and I live it.

"Metro New York," 9/22/11 posted a blurb: "NYPD WARNS OF CLUB TERROR." I love it. Bring it on. Didn't everybody read *1984*? *Brave New World*? Lots of us were aware of the misuse and abuse of totally fabricated "TERROR ALERTS" during the Bush elections. Bill Maher and others (probably Michael Moore) commented on them freely. "Be Scared!" the government said. "We will protect you!" Better yet, *you* protect *us*. Enlist! It's classic macho bullshit. "Don't worry, little lady, I'll take care of you." America as John Wayne. America as "john," period.

So the "Metro NY" piece says: "The NYPD doesn't think any place in the city is safe from terrorism, even a thumping nightclub. After clubs were bombed overseas in recent years (that's recent?) from London to Bali, the NYPD is concerned that a suicide bomber might try to do the same in a Manhattan bar. The police department issued its 'best practices for nightlife establishments' this week and warned bar owners to be prepared. The guide encourages owners to have a terrorism emergency plan in place. Police even suggested that bartenders and bouncers be on the lookout for possible suicide bombers, who may be concealing their hands or look nervous." (Because everyone else in bars is totally relaxed with no hands in their pockets?)

As if bouncers don't have enough to worry about with drunks, drugs, and guns. Now they're on terror alert, working unofficially (and unpaid) for the government? "If you see something, say something" has been the New York City slogan since 9/11. I think: "Officer, I see trash all around and lots of homeless people in despair." Regarding refuse on the subways the poster reads: "Don't assume it was left by accident!" No? Now every derelict piece of luggage or jettisoned brown paper bag is a potential bomb. The dark powers that be are trying to instill and sustain a "state of fear" to keep us small and make sure their big guns get bigger.

I say, go to the club and have fun. Take the train and celebrate. Go to work and claim your day in joy. Rebuff "their" invitation to imbibe fear, the elixir of disempowerment. Rebuff their fascist propaganda to stay small, to let "big brother" take care of you, and of course, to hate the invisible (and ever-changing) enemy. Don't drink the Kool-Aid. Who *are* "they" you ask? Anyone who sells fear to the masses. This is the Age of Aquarius and we are here to drink the waters of life, not death. We are here to enjoy peace, not submit to fear. Identify and ignore the fear-mongers. They are dinosaurs, and they are dying.

You go to that club, dance, have fun, then go home and celebrate your life and your freedom, which no one can take from you unless you willingly give it. If you want to stay safe, use a condom. Don't drink and drive. Try to like, and God forbid, love, the person you're sleeping with. Claim your God-given right to uplift yourself through prayer, meditation, right-thinking, right-living, and the empowerment of your Self as a Divine Being Living in Human Form. Amen.

CHAPTER 2

LABEL ME DUMB

October 5, 2011

Whine alert! I'm about to rant. What's in a name? What's underneath the label? In our label obsessed world Tiffany's makes eyeglasses, and I'm convinced that diapers by LaCoste are not far behind. People used to want an education, now they want the $7,000 (or is it more by now?) Birkin bag. Since we equate money with success, no wonder we've lost our moral bearings and are ruining our environment, not to mention our lives. No worries if someone is shallow or ruthless, if they're good-looking, we give them a reality show.

Fran Lebowitz was interviewed in an article about "Sin" in *Vogue* magazine years ago. She talked about Claus

Von Bulow, who was acquitted of attempting to murder his wife. She said that in the old days, bad people were shunned. Today, they are given the best tables in our finest restaurants. We're so fame–obsessed, we'll even settle for infamy. In our shallow culture, image is all and content be damned. We've been living on a diet of marshmallow "Fluff" and wonder why we feel sick. Shopping and plastic surgery cannot fill that insatiable void.

Chris Rock made a wonderful film about black hair called *Good Hair*, in which he documents the lengths that (mostly) women (and Al Sharpton) go to to "relax," enhance, or replace what nature gave them. He concludes his film by telling his young daughters (who ask early in the film why they "don't have good hair") that's he's more concerned with what's *in* their head than what's *on* it.

Chris Bell's documentary *Bigger, Stronger, Faster* is about our obsession with looks and fame (he focuses on men, sports, and steroids). Men have succumbed to our culture's obsession with superficiality as surely as women. This mindset correlates to the disposable nature of our products, our voracious appetite for more, newer, and of course, bigger. A friend of mine bought a brand new near-million-dollar suburban home maybe fifteen years ago. It sported a plain cement walkway to the "grand" entrance. A mil didn't even buy her a pretty brick path. Her two-year-old daughter ripped the toilet paper holder out of the sheetrock wall within one week. But it looked great. A great big doll's house.

While sitting in a very crowded Second Avenue bus years ago, I was assaulted by a large stomach. It extended out from under a guy's tee shirt and into my personal space. He had lots of hardware hanging off of him, so I concluded he was a plumber. His ass attempted an escape from its denim girdle as he twisted through the aisles to exit. When he turned, I caught an unwanted glimpse of his buttocks, trying to make the break from their textile jail. His underwear peered out, screaming to be noticed so we could give him the appropriate fashion credit for wearing Calvin Klein. Calvin, now available at Costco, used to stand for class. Now he markets to the masses. I mean asses. Cash is king.

I'm baffled by the vast number of white people changing their names to things like Mahasatvaa Ma Ananda Sarita, PhD. I know a young woman who has changed her perfectly lovely name three times since I met her five years ago. Who is she? I'm sure she can't tell us. However, I fully support my friend who legally changed her middle name from Anne to Jane because her initials *used* to spell F.A.T. How could her parents not have figured that one out? And why does everybody have to have THREE names these days? Are we all Jacqueline *Bouvier* Kennedy? I admit I use my first and middle names on Facebook because my full name was already taken by a lovely tattoo artist in California (and several other shameless Valerie Gilbert impersonators).

I know "Drs." who are neither medical professionals nor PhDs. One has a full-page ad in a new age rag. This

"Dr." is a "Mega Super Star World Famous Clairvoyant" who charges $2,500 per hour (yes, your eyes are working). He offers the "path to enlightenment" but "needs your help" to raise $2.5 million (you read that right, too) to build his "Temple of Divine Prophecy." It's a non-profit, of course. He'll help you "if you need more money, a new job, or a healing." Can't he give himself a session? I'll tell you what he needs. Some clothing. He's wrapped in a large diaper in the ad, striking a Pharoahnic pose. He also needs a real job, though I suspect the one he has now is quite lucrative.

Remember when stewardesses became flight attendants? Secretaries became assistants? And when "The Jefferson's" housekeeper Florence announced that she wasn't a maid, but a "household engineer?" I was frequently employed as a secretary and called myself one simply because I was sick of all the fancifying and faux upgrading. No one is a writer anymore, they are a *bestselling* author or *internationally* known speaker, world famous teacher, or reality show STAR, the superlatives never end. Everyone is desperate to be the *best*. Life has become a TV contest.

I want to know why Michael Jackson wore epaulets. Was he in the military? Was he royalty? Yes, by our crazy standards, rock and roll royalty, which is why he got away with all the madness until it killed him. God knows what it did to all those little boys he had "sleepovers" with. Was he massively talented and charismatic? Yes. An alien? Probably. Those beefed up militarized space outfits gave him a puffed up sense of power, and, unfortunately, a false sense of immunity and entitlement. Perhaps it's the same with people's bloated biceps and ginormous breasts. Why does everyone have to be bigger than life? What's wrong with life size?

People are desperate to be loved. There's no fix for that except to love and accept ourselves as we are. Go ahead, dye your hair and work out at the gym. Bathing, a *great* idea. Better yet is a healthy self-esteem, something no Botox, Restalyn, steroids, epaulets, or titles can give you. Be yourself. Be. Just live. Know that this is blessing enough. Claim your heritage as a Divine Child. God don't need no designer jeans!

Who is beneath the husband, father, employee, son, consumer, fan, and stamp collector? Now that's a mystery worth exploring. We are not our resumes. I embrace the Fool, the first card in the Tarot deck. She's the explorer, the naïf. I remain curious, ever-changing, and indefinable, a mystery rather than a well-read book or a person who can be categorized and reduced to a few credentials or sound bites.

Reverend Billy's Earthalujiah mission and his Church of "Stop Shopping!" (he hilariously calls our culture's obsession with acquisition "The Shopacalypse") has the antidote: stop shopping, start loving. We must start with ourselves. People before things.

John Perkins, author of *Confessions of an Economic Hit Man* writes that we have an amazing new capacity to communicate with (almost) everyone around the world via technology. "Will we continue to use our ability to communicate to talk about fashion, sports, and the love lives of movie stars? Or will we tell our corporate & political leaders that we insist on an economy driven by commitment to providing everyone with adequate food, shelter, social services; cleaning up the polluted air, land, & water; developing efficient forms of transportation; reducing energy consumption & redirecting it to sustainable technologies?"

Call me deaf, dumb, and blind. I just wanna BE. We are, you know, Free to Be. You and Me.

CHAPTER 3

STACKING THE DECK

October 9, 2011

Someone gave me a craptacular tarot deck. While the artwork wasn't bad and it came in a pretty, diaphanous, purple bag, it was impossible to decipher. I don't read tarot well on a good day. I have to look up each and every card, and the flimsy pamphlet that came with my Aquarian deck is basic, to say the least. But I like the *idea* of tarot cards. They are mysterious, and depending on which version you have, quite beautiful.

This gift deck had new suits. Made up suits. Instead of the standard Wands, Swords, Cups and Pentacles, it had Shells (what the f'?) Gems, Roses, and Wings. I ask you. Tarot is inscrutable enough without me having to translate cups into wings and swords into roses. But the deck was pretty enough that I kept it lying around, and I started using a card or two as bookmarks, at which they excelled. There was no need to interpret the card now. We both knew what it meant once it was lodged firmly in a tome. Sit! Stay! Keep that book in line! It wasn't telling *me* what was what anymore, I was telling *it*. The dynamics of our relationship had started to change.

I pull a single card from this sketchy deck (and several other premonitory decks) to start the day for a simple, New-York-minute reading. I don't have the patience or skills for a full spread. I have Celtic cards, angel cards, Archangel Michael cards, animal cards. Usually a single card will suffice. I say, "Tell me what I need to know today," et voila, a revealing message ensues.

Right before I allowed an acquaintance to stay with me for a few days I woke up with Lindsey Buckingham's song "Trouble" in my head. This didn't bode well although I love the song, so I decided to look up the lyrics. It's a love song. The guy's in trouble because he's falling in love. I sighed with relief, although I wasn't looking to fall in love with my friend. But then I pulled an animal card, Coyote, the trickster, which implies the potential for manipulation or trouble. Turned out the title of the song *and* the card was right, or rather my intuition, which they both reflected, was right. The four-day visit ended explosively. I patted my intuition on its back and sighed with more relief that the guest was gone. I felt empowered that the signs I'd received were accurate.

I pulled three cards for a coaching client from my fragmentary deck (remember, I had a few cards deployed as bookmarks) before I started working with her. I pulled Anxiety, Perfectionism, and Independence prior to her arrival. Anxiety was worrisome but accurate. Perfectionism, too, turned out to be correct. She was a perfectionist and short-circuited herself from trying things (and potentially looking the fool) as a result. Instead, she remained frozen perfectly in place, a position I never advocate unless wild dogs are sniffing you. And finally, Independence, what I hoped to achieve in my coaching work with her.

Another day a medium friend of mine grabbed the fractional deck to give herself a reading. I warned her, "It's incomplete! Sundry cards are hiding in books around the house!" She didn't care and was very satisfied with the results of her redacted reading.

But then I took to putting cards back into the half-assed deck and arguing with them when I didn't like their message. "Anxiety? That's not how I want to start the day! What a downer. In fact, how *rude*!" I'm not going to let a painted, plastic-coated piece of cardboard plant a dark seed in my head. I decide how I react to the things that happen to me. I'm the captain of my ship. Even if a day is troublesome I don't have to choose anxiety as a response. Yes, I believe we have control over this; that our thoughts create our feelings and our beliefs create the attitudes that inform our days.

If I picked yet *another* foreboding card, I'd toss it away in disgust then toss another and another until I was finally granted a more promising card. This was a strangely empowering practice, looking first to the cards for direction but then decreeing, "I will not submit to your dark and capricious whims, you pile of dried wood pulp." The Archangel Michael deck never gives me depressing feedback. The worst he does is look like Fabio on the cover of a romance novel (and I've already spoken to him about *that*). The angel cards never disappoint. Their messages are nurturing and inspirational. I'm looking for divination, not damnation, dammit!

Finally, I decided to audit the errant deck outright once and for all. I made three piles: *Excellent* (happy) cards, *Metza Metz* cards like "Work" (who wants to wake up to that?) and *Downright Awful Cards*. This last category included: Obsession (what I had for the unbalanced men I used to date who left me feeling...unbalanced), Fear, The Realist (how depressing), Frustration (right on!), Sacrifice (I'm neither Abraham nor Mother Theresa, thank you very much), Competition (don't like it), Crisis (I've had enough), Perfectionism (an annoying trait), Disappointment, Sorrow, Opposition, Defeat, Indecision, Anxiety, Habits, Stress, Difficulty, and Possessiveness. I tossed the Metza Metz and Downright Awfuls into the recycling bin.

What a sense of power! I felt liberated from a ridiculously small prison, "a house of cards," if you will, but a prison nonetheless. I decided to toss the "bad news" bookmarks, too, since I read books on how to uplift my energies physically, emotionally, mentally, and spiritually. I don't want downer energy in my books, my bed, my home, or my life. Someone should make a "Bad News Tarot" deck for the melancholic that prefer a dose of "reality." Some people are happy to be unhappy.

Are you stacking *your* deck in your favor? Do you surround yourself with supportive and loving people? Do they enhance your sparkle? Do they believe in you and let you know? Do you love and support *them?* (Respect is best when it goes both ways.) Love supports and inflates. It does not tear down and deflate. Look around you. Look *inside* you. Are you happy? If not, why not? Now, go do something about it. It's your party.

I *defy* "The Realist" card (formerly of my questionable deck). I live firmly in the world. It is black and white, with a lot of gray. I know fresh snow turns yellow, gray, then black in short order in New York City. I know people lose jobs. I've lost them. I know people die. I've lost them, too. I know there's a recession, and that I have moods that are not always sunny, and I honor those shadow moods like I honor the moon, although the more I prioritize and safeguard my happiness, the happier I've become. I've refused to go back to office jobs that were soul killing. I haven't dated dark, angry, unreliable types in years.

Yes, it's *my* tarot deck, ladies and gentlemen, and when I discarded those depressing cards, all that they represented went away: depressing jobs, depressing friends, disappointing lovers. Whatever you're willing to put up with is exactly what you'll get. I've set my bar higher. I'm not settling anymore. Are you?

Do you know which cards I'm left with after my Tarot Bloodbath? Romance, Motivation, Victory, Fulfillment, Creativity, Power, Tradition, Vision, Passion, Balance, Privacy, Independence, Nurture, Seduction, The Mover, The Adventurer, Consummation, Perspective, Attraction, Joy, The Professional, Illusion, Celebration, Passage, Energy, Determination, Attitude, Success, Love, Protection, The Ingénue, The Builder, Introspection, Understanding, Trust, Patience, The Leader, Change, The Messenger, Triumph, Intuition, The Charmer, Reward, Support, The Analyst, Respect, Truth, The Challenger, Re-Evaluation, Hope, Luck, Generosity, Opportunity, and Transformation.

Now, that's a stacked deck I can live with! Editing your life doesn't have to mean you're delusional or hiding from things. It just means *you get to pick*. Don't put up with shit. Don't settle for less. Don't postpone joy. And if you want to know how synchronicity works, or "being in the vortex" according to Abraham-Hicks (a channeling team) look at what I just found on the internet, in Bridgett Walther's astrological report for me this week, starting today:

"You make a conscious choice (this is empowerment in its noblest form) *to attract positive energy* and to deflect all things negative. You erase negativity from your mind because it causes stress, fine lines, less energy, and attracts very problematic, manipulative people with too many neurotic complications. Focus on what is beautiful, full of life and love, and rewarding. Since you've decided to view life from a funny, ironic, playful side, you'll feel as if a door has been opened and cool, fresh, brisk air blasts in, erasing all the negative elements you've toted around far too long. Start practicing this new approach to living by avoiding jaded pessimists and sardonic self-proclaimed geniuses. Keep practicing your new attitude every day and you could have this new way of living, thinking, and loving down to a science."

Yes, ladies and gentlemen. I am starting to live in *my* vortex, the delicious, cream-filled center of Who I Am, of Who We All Are, Love Incarnate. Love in the flesh. We are the Word of God. By banishing the dust and detritus of the past *and* present, we embrace a brilliant new future beyond our wildest imaginings. If you were dealt "a bad hand" then throw out those naughty cards and buy some new ones!

CHAPTER 4

BEES WAX

October 19, 2011

New York Magazine recently had a cover story on older moms entitled, "Is She Just Too Old For This?" I'm pretty sure they superimposed an older, white-haired female head on a younger, pregnant, female body, producing a shot akin to Demi Moore's shocking *Vanity Fair* cover crossed with something from AARP. Actually, on second look I see that it is an older-ish body too, with a firm, very pregnant protruding belly superimposed in the middle. I suspect that the cover model, who looks 60 plus not the 50 they talk about in the article, was knocked up by Photoshop.

The article is about the ethics of choosing to be an older parent. Can we talk about the ethics of parenting, period? Is it selfish to want a child, whether biological or adopted, knowing that "the clock is ticking" and that you may not be there to see them graduate, wed, breed, etc? Isn't all parenting selfish? Let's look at the motivations: How many people have a baby to "save" their marriage? We know how well that one works. How many young women have a baby to keep or entrap a man? How many teenaged girls have babies so they will have someone to love them (yes, this is the rationale for many, as if the child is a puppy, and everyone with a puppy knows just how much work it requires). How many men want children to prove their virility, to prove they are straight, or because it's expected of them by their parents, family or friends?

How about dead-beat dads who abandon their kids? How about men who want their women pregnant and cooking? They're not proving their masculinity for the child's sake. What's their motivation for breeding? To pass on a name, a business, a tradition? To create "immortality" for their DNA, followers for their religion? Is that proper motivation? How about women who leave their babies in dumpsters or men who beat or kill their wives and babies. They're better than the older couple with security?

Why was the Octomom allowed to breed (with state funding) with her atrocious breeding record and a total staggering spawn count of *fourteen*? Why did people look to "Jon and Kate and Their 8" as admirable or interesting in any way? Was there any parenting going on, or just grandstanding?

Bill Maher said, "Humans were not meant to be born in litters." I'm with Bill. Octuplets are the new DD fake breasts, the Hummers of childbirth. Where did simplicity go? We're so greedy; buy more, breed more, do what you want, it's a free country. But not when it comes to older moms. We judge them to be selfish, pretending to be something they're not. Young.

A good friend of mine is a midwife. She counseled a fifteen-year-old to terminate her early pregnancy because, well, being a mom at 15 just didn't seem like a great idea. Just because your body is capable of reproducing doesn't mean your psyche is. Her very Catholic grandmother was with the girl at the clinic. My friend gave the child a prescription for an abortion pill. Months later the same little girl came in again with her abuela for a prenatal checkup. My friend asked her why she hadn't taken the pill. The girl said "I couldn't afford $26 for the prescription." Of course! And taking care of a child for eighteen years will be *so* much cheaper…Is this *child* a better candidate for motherhood than some older broad who really wants one?

What of teenage couples who think they can handle parenthood while attending (or dropping out of) high school? What about single moms by choice? I've heard them described (by a man) as totally selfish for consciously depriving their kid of a dad.

I know of worse situations. I know kids whose dads were present but not fathers. They were neither nurturing, loving nor attentive. Some of them were sexually abusive. My high school friend's divorced dad was dating an 18 year old when we were 17. Creepy! I only visited her at her mom's house. Who would want to hang out with a dad who views you as a potential date? I know kids whose parents were nasty, abusive, alcoholic, drug-addicted, porn-addicted, and workaholics. I know a dad who couldn't pay the rent and who hit up my friend, a fourth grader, for cigarette money. She couldn't sleep nights because she worried they'd be on the streets soon. So, what was *his* solution? He left the family and started another one out in Colorado. Right on! There are parents busy saving the world who ignore their families. Parents who care about causes or business but not people, certainly not their own children. There are parents who are sick, and parents who die. How's that for selfish?

And what of people who use their kids as accessories the way Brittney Spears used to tote her toy chihuahua around? To quote Bill Maher again, what does a photo of a smiling politician and his wife and kids prove? "Oh, good, his *dick* works." It doesn't mean he's a good dad, or a good person, or that they're a happy or even functional family. Look at Maria Shriver and her "Ahnold." Now there's a selfless husband and father. Our culture is dictated by Toys R' Us superficiality and stupidity. If the photo looks good, it must be real.

Something about a 50-plus-year-old woman having a baby just doesn't look right, does it? We like our women young. Our mothers young. Our sex objects young, and if not young, then *looking* young. It's all about appearances. It's hard not to reduce this issue to pure sexism and ageism. Men sire children into their 80's. No one much cares so long as they leave some cash behind along with their sperm. It puts me in the mind of the fantastic film *Harold and Maude* when military man Uncle Victor chastises young Harold for sleeping with octogenarian Maude:

> "You have a very common neurosis, particularly in this society, whereby the male child subconsciously wishes to sleep with his mother. Of course, what puzzles me, Harold, is that you want to sleep with your grandmother. I would be remiss in my duty if I did not tell you that the idea of…intercourse…and the fact of your firm, young body co-mingling with her withered flesh, sagging breasts, and flabby buttocks…makes me want to vomit."

My parents were in their forties when I was born. I was a "surprise." They had my sister in their thirties and wanted more kids, but none came until my last minute appearance. I was welcome, but unexpected. People act like it's strange or shocking for someone to have a child in their forties or fifties. It is not. They used to be called "change of life" babies. Even peri-menopausal women can conceive naturally. If women and men want to play around with science regarding their fertility, which I personally wouldn't, it's their choice. I don't want plastic surgery, either. Frankly, I'm not big on doctors, period. I go for vitamins, herbs and acupuncture.

So Much, So Fast is a documentary about the most beautiful family solidarity and love. Of three sons, one of them develops ALS (Lou Gehrig's disease) in his twenties. A good looking guy, Stephen gets sick, falls in love, gets married, and asks his wife to have his baby. She agrees. His disease progresses throughout. Doctors figure he has about five years to live, average for sufferers of the disease. Baby Alex is the light of his life. They try to have a second kid, even as Stephen's disease continues to incapacitate him with ever increasing alacrity. Was it selfish for him to father a child knowing he would die soon? I believe his son Alex is a very lucky boy. He was born to two parents who adored each other, and who adored him. He is part of an extended family that nurtured Stephen, his wife, and his kid. This is one big, loving family. How many kids get a beautiful start like that in life? I'm putting my money on little Alex Heywood.

When he died, Stephen Heywood was 38. Randy Pausch (*The Last Lecture*) was 48. Steve Jobs was 56. We come with no guarantees in life, though everyone seems to feel entitled to fame, health, wealth, success, big houses, big families, and long life. We want it all in this country. We don't get it all, or, as comedian Steven Wright said, "You can't have it all. Where would you put it?" We are not ensured long life. We are not guaranteed happiness, though in this country we were once promised the ability to pursue it among many other rights that have since been "alienably" stripped by the brutish Bush regime.

We cling to life because we are afraid of death. We cling to science as a defense against decay. Women die in childbirth. Fathers plain old die. Kids are born sick. We act as if the template for everyone is cyber health and perpetual physical life. It is not. So if you don't want older gals to conceive, use a surrogate, or adopt, then tell young gals who are ill-equipped to parent (and are more likely to abuse, abandon, or kill their spawn) that they can't have babies either. Tell dads they're not allowed to split and not support their children. Tell moms they're not allowed to be depressed, angry, or conflicted, or feed their kids junk and fast "foods."

If a kid has *one* loving and reliable adult in their life they are very, *very* lucky. It might be a parent. It could be a grandparent. A school teacher. A neighbor. It could be a dog, cat, or hamster. When it comes to who decides to bring a child into this world and when, I say let the old broads do what they want and mind your bees wax.

CHAPTER 5

FINDING GARDENS

October 25, 2011

A friend of mine called the other afternoon. "Oh, this is nice. This is really nice. I can't believe I've never seen this before!"

"Where are you?" I asked.

"Central Park, 105th Street and Fifth Ave."

"Oooh," I said knowingly. "The Conservatory Garden, isn't it gorgeous? Don't you *love* the flowers?"

"There aren't any flowers. It's October," she replied.

I said, "Well, don't you love the statues and the fountains?"

"There aren't any statues or fountains," she replied.

"Yes there are! Look around."

She wandered around a bit further then gasped, "Ooh…oh! Look at that!"

"What do you see?" I asked.

"There *are* flowers!" she said. "Wait, there's a statue. And a fountain! Oh my God. I'm in Heaven." She had become Alice in Wonderland.

For those of you who've not been to the Conservatory Garden in New York City it's like being transported to France whilst yards away from the M1 bus and The Barrio Museum. As you step deeper and deeper into this sacred space, Versailles comes very much into focus. It is a formal garden, the kind kings and queens and the very, very rich have, tucked just inside Central Park, and adjacent to bustling Fifth Avenue traffic.

My friend's life is in stark contrast to this garden. She is a single mom. Her husband ditched her and their kid when the child was five, complete with no child support (we lovingly refer to him as "a deadbeat dad"). He moved to Florida with his hoochie mama and gave *her* a big fat diamond ring. The one he never gave his wife of thirteen years.

She has worked for the City of New York since she was eighteen. It is many decades later now. She manages three housing projects in Harlem and is the director of two thousand apartments, an accomplishment to be very proud of. There is no glory associated with this achievement. There is drama, dirt, vermin, stress from the bureaucracy, deadbeat tenants, whiners, trash, more trash, lack of staff, lack of money, people who do nothing, and things that never get done. And let's not forget the cops, the dead bodies, and the occasional fire or two. She cares too much about her tenants and her staff. She does too much for her family, friends, and co-workers. Her feet hurt. Her head hurts. Her back hurts. Her heart could be in better shape. I want Calgon to take her away.

My fantasy for this big-hearted friend who regularly gives her last dollar away—and who is generous with her food, her time, her ear, and her love—my fantasy for this friend is that she will find a man someday who will take care of her. Considering that no one has taken good care of her since early youth, that she was a latchkey kid, that she has *always* supported herself, and often supported her men, this is not a sexist, passive conceit. She's a workhorse and commutes two hours each day between Manhattan and Long Island. She gives and gives and gives. I want her to receive. But I can't stop her from picking the men she has picked, like the one who tried to kill her and the other one (or two) who just hit her.

The last fellow she dated seemed a decent sort, though I never met him. He was so similar to her that even their first names, ages, and marital status (single, one teenaged kid) were almost identical. They both worked for the city. They probably made around the same amount of money. She liked him, but he slunk away after five months or so. My friend was thrown because she was starting to trust him and to believe that he was a decent man. She claimed she was upset by his text message that ended it all. But she wasn't upset. First of all, she wasn't in love with him. I think she liked him because he seemed to like her. That's not the same thing as really liking someone. It's trying to second-guess a situation. When you pick someone for rational reasons, it usually blows up in your face. The reason you should pick someone is because you like them. Well, heck, *you* decide the reason you want to be with someone. Some people like partners because they are dangerous. Unhinged. Unbalanced. When Carrie Fisher's alter-ego Suzanne says in *Postcards from the Edge* she likes "interesting" men, interesting means "problems."

My friend broke up a million and one times with the guy who tried to kill her. One of those fucked-up situations where the adrenaline and addiction to drama was so strong that she was literally a junkie for this man, swearing she was over him again and again then reaching out to him the next day. Or caving-in to him when he beseeched her. I was dizzy from hearing about all the back and forth. "I'm over it!" "I saw him…" "I hate him!" "I saw him…" It was a merry-go-round on speed. It took years for her to finally sever the ties. For real.

So this latest fellow, the one who seemed nice but was ultimately disappointing, and her sadness and surprise when he pulled back, this was nothing. She called it depression but she wasn't strung out. He wasn't a lunatic, and she wasn't his shrieking vampirette. She was okay. She was more than okay. So she gained a couple of pounds.

After listening to her for years with loser after loser, she finally hit a sort of parity with this last one. A parity within herself. This pleasant but unremarkable relationship ended quietly. Maturely. She did not fall apart. And so, on a fine October day in New York City, she wandered down south from Harlem at lunch and found herself, magically, in The Secret Garden of Central Park.

"There's a butterfly! It's coming near me! It almost landed on me!" She was like a child. She was exploring new territory in this series of gardens that reflected Italian, English, and French styles within the conservatory. "I'm in Heaven." Yes, she was. That garden has been there for decades, but she didn't find it until today. She *couldn't* have found it until today. She didn't have eyes to see beauty or the heart to feel peace.

A few days later she went to my chiropractor for the first time. I'd implored her for years to try this gentle healer, a man who understands the holistic nature of well-being. Dr. William Zev Roizer is a miracle worker and a kind, generous, and talented man. My friend was in agony. She suffered from such profound job stress—coupled with the stress from her 88-year-old mother getting into a car accident—that she could barely walk. Desperation drove her to my doctor. Whatever it took, I was grateful she was there.

Her mom is out of the hospital and in rehab. And who was in the rehab center but a very cute doctor. Nothing wrong with the blue-collar types my friend used to be attracted to (actually, there was *everything* wrong with the specific guys she picked) but would it hurt her to like a doctor for a change? A guy who actually *takes care* of people?

I keep dreaming about her Mr. Right, her Prince Charming. I don't believe everyone deserves one. I believe she deserves one. And *she* was starting to believe that she deserved one. We don't get what we deserve. We get what we *think* we deserve. Whatever we're willing to put up with is exactly what we get.

She's starting to see herself with new eyes. She's starting to feel herself in new ways. She's happier than she's ever been. She's losing weight. She told her nutritionist to go screw herself (not exactly, but she stopped going when this woman continued to insist that my friend exercise at *least* an hour daily and eat no more than 1000 calories a day). Leave the torture to the Middle Ages, okay? She didn't drop a pound under this expert "supervision."

When we are miserable we create more misery. Now that she is pulling herself out of her mental and emotional muck, she is stepping into new terrain. Terrain where people smile at her, like her, treat her well and give her things. She just won the cash prize in a raffle last week, $283 bucks! What can I say? Happiness heals. She is finding gardens because she is growing them.

CHAPTER 6

THE BUCK STOPS HERE

October 30, 2011

What would it be like to live in a world of total transparency? To know that when you buy corn, it is natural, not genetically modified? To know that when a mass-produced cereal claims to be made with honey, that it's not a commercial version of "honey" purchased at 19 cents a pound from China and diluted with sugar syrup? (Rent the documentary *The Vanishing of the Bees*.) That when a politician says he will do something he actually does it? Radical.

A person's word used to mean something; deals were made on handshakes. Integrity = integer = whole. When our word matches our deed we have integrity. If someone says "I'm going to kill you," and they do it, they have integrity, just no morals. (I'm playing!) Don Miguel Ruiz directs us in *The Four Agreements* to always be impeccable with our word.

Don't listen to what people say. Watch what they do. Until their words match their deeds (integrity) what they do *is* who they are. "I really wanted to come…" "Oh, I *meant* to get it for you." "Let's have lunch." "I'll call you!" Unless they follow up on these empty words, often said to appease, to lubricate the social cogs, to "seem" nice, they are liars. Sound extreme? I disagree. Try it on as truth. We make far too many excuses for people and, in the process, we don't help them, or ourselves. While I'm at it, what does the word "try" mean? "I'll *try* to come." It means they won't come. So, "I'll try" is another lie, albeit a white one. If you're really unsure, why not say "I doubt I'll make it, but thanks for the invitation." It's clean.

In attempts to cover their asses, people fib, fudge, and fabricate. Has anyone taken responsibility for the financial malfeasance that has wreaked havoc on our country and the world's economy? Have you heard a *one* of them say, "I fucked up"? Ah, no. Because in their minds, they *didn't* fuck up. They just got caught. They got rich via others' ruination. Since they're narcissists, they don't care about those people "out there" (I mean "down there," actually, I mean "what people?"). They're not remorseful beyond the fact that they're now in trouble. Most of them still have no clue how the other half, I'm sorry, the other 99%, lives.

Which leads me to the Madoffs, and for those who like word play and symbolism as I do, just look at their *name*. They *made off* with the money! I was amused by recent pieces about them in the media due to Ruth's *60 Minutes* interview tonight. Ruth says they *tried* (there's that word again) to kill themselves because their guilt and the hatred from others was too much. Well, they didn't *try* hard enough, did they? "I don't know whose idea it was (You don't? Seems a pretty powerful suggestion to forget who thought of it) but we decided to kill ourselves because it was so horrendous *what was happening.*" What *was* happening, Ruth?

She made it sound as if what was happening *had nothing to do with them*. What was "happening" was a reaction to what they *did*. They bilked people out of billions of dollars and the hatred directed toward them was the direct result of their actions. The Madoffs' attitude seems to be "What? We didn't *mean* to hurt anybody." I don't believe they were trying to hurt anybody, any more than the corrupt power brokers (and I don't believe that all power brokers are necessarily corrupt) are trying to hurt people. They just don't give a shit. Being sociopathic narcissists, all they care about is that they get theirs (and everybody else's).

The Madoffs don't feel guilty about what they did. They had no guilt while they were perpetrating the fraud, did they? Were there sleep issues? Skin breakouts? Indigestion? I haven't heard of any. The guilt came only because they got caught. They feel bad because they are in trouble and the hatred, disdain, and disgust from others is galling to them because they had a childish need to be loved, admired, and looked up to. As if wealth is something to be proud of. I am all for abundance if it is honestly earned, but having cash in and of itself is not a noble quality any more than having a full head of hair is.

Bernie and Ruth were upset by the "terrible phone calls, hate mail, just beyond anything…" How *could* their victims be so cruel? They felt they couldn't go on anymore, while their victims were forced to (sans their fortunes). Their attempt to kill themselves on Christmas Eve "made it all the more depressing," she said. They couldn't enjoy their eggnog or Christmas prezzies! Boo hoo. They have no concern at all for what they put their victims through. Now, *that* would be guilt. The Madoffs feel sorry for themselves and that's it. They haven't repented. No moral light bulb has gone off in their heads or hearts. The fact that they mailed her valuable jewelry to family members before their suicide attempt and not to lawyers to distribute to their victims proves their lack of willingness to make reparations.

The Madoffs act as if they are being put-upon, as if they are the victims and not the perpetrators. I assert that they are unhappy, self-hating people. Just because they're narcissists doesn't mean they're not self-hating. Narcissism has nothing to do with the healthy self-love that I advocate. These were never happy, healthy, loving people. They were operating from the lowest common denominators of human behavior: lust, greed and avarice in the guise of wealth, power, and "success." We as a culture are now in the process of redefining those very terms. What is wealth and success if it comes at the expense of others' lives, livelihoods, freedoms, and happiness?

What if everyone told the truth? What if *you* spoke your mind and heart without the fear of repercussions? What if corporations and governments did the same? Can you feel the beauty in that? Visualize *that* world for just a moment. Now, go and make it happen by standing in your light and truth. The world will catch on. That's right, *we're* the leaders! From your tiny corner of the world, contemplate the grandness of Your Being. We are not specks. We are Spectacular!

The Madoffs of this world are dying. We are coming into our Own. It is Our Time.

Starr Fuentes, a Polish-Mexican witch with a raucous sense of humor asserts, "When you lie, your aura dims." Not everybody can see auras. Some people can. Animals can. Lots of people walk around sporting a dark cloud like Pig Pen from *Peanuts*. This goes for white lies, too. Why do we have such an aversion to speaking the truth? Probably from being burned at the stake in past lives or dying to defend the truth for a noble cause. And also from the fact that 90% of our culture is predicated on lies and deceit and that we think it's normal and okay to cheat on everything from our taxes to our spouses. Of course the fact that our government and Corporations (the *real* government) lie and cheat doesn't help anything, does it? Where *does* the buck stop?

I would like to trust my government. Right now, I don't, but it's getting better because WE THE PEOPLE are claiming our voice, power, and authority once more. We've learned that trusting and expecting Big Brother to take care of us eviscerates, disempowers, and turns us into children. When we fight back to reclaim our planet, our resources, and our autonomy we claim our true legacy as Beings of Light.

We don't yet live in a world where everyone is accepted for who they are but we can change that by accepting *ourselves* for who we are, now. Advocate for yourself by standing in your light and speaking your truth. Imagine being fully known for who you really are. No more secrets, no more lies. For those in the know about chakras, our lower three are being phased out during the ascension process. They'll be a vestigial tail before long. Survival as an M.O. is on the outs. We're leaving "fight or flight" in the dust. Love will be our new baseline as we stop struggling and start to thrive (aaaahhh…wrap your smile around that one!) The heart chakra will be the new root. Above the heart, a *truth* chakra is evolving. It is turquoise, a blend between the green of the heart (love) and the blue of the throat (communication). Truth is the child of love and expression. When you are living fully in your truth, this chakra will activate and you will not be able to lie. You will also know when anyone else is lying.

I was coaching someone and followed up with her about something she'd agreed to do. She paused, then calmly and coolly said, "It didn't happen."

I said, "Well, was it supposed to happen by itself? Or were you supposed to do it? How about claiming responsibility for what didn't happen. *That* sentence would sound like 'I didn't do it.' It's really important to take responsibility for what you do and to speak the truth. Go on…say it."

She looked at me warily then spoke. "Okay, I didn't do it."

I smiled and hugged her. "Great! Great! It's the truth."

She didn't do it because she didn't want to—plain and simple. We do what we want to do. Some take issue with that concept, insisting that there are many things we don't want to do but *have* to. We disempower ourselves when we choose to believe that. Even if you do something you "don't" want to do (i.e. prepare your taxes), you still make the decision that it is better for you to do it than to not do it. You want what is best for yourself so you do the thing you "didn't want to do." Your wanting may be of a different nature when avoiding pain than it is when eating cake, but it still comes from desire. That desire is to take care of yourself.

We are all doing the best we can all the time based on our beliefs. No one sets out to fuck up. And if we do, it's because we believe there's some benefit to "fucking up." For instance, "Now I can *prove* I'm a loser and Mom and Dad will leave me alone!" Did Bernie and Ruth set out to hurt people and cause their own ruination? Absolutely not. Do I think what they did was okay? Of course not. And that's why karma and the law exist. To set boundaries for those who don't respectfully set them for themselves and to curtail behaviors that are malignant toward society.

How's this for another definition of integrity: our choices not only benefit ourselves but the society and planet that supports our very being? What if corporations and governments operated that way and *cooperated* instead of competed? What if we held a "Whole World Pot Luck Dinner," bringing our gifts to the table, and benefiting from the beauty and magnificence of that great and varied spread? Symbiosis. Living together, benefiting, and helping each other. Being helped, loved, and supported in return. Feeling safe. Visualize that. Now Make It Happen. The Buck Stops Here. What Happens Next is Up to You.

CHAPTER 7

ROCK...PAPER...SCISSORS

November 6, 2011

I took a seminar with an Irish Guru who shall remain nameless. When I first saw a photo of him in a book, I was mesmerized by his loving gaze and couldn't believe the energy that seemed to jump off the page from his gorgeous face. Later in that same book there was a photo of this guru's guru, an Indian dude, decidedly ungorgeous but also with the most searing gaze and love seemingly popping off the page and into my pores. What was going on?

I was intrigued with this Irish character but turned off when I attended an event of his in the city. His acolytes were weird. Unfriendly. And the music was loud. The meditations were corny. Irish Dude wasn't there but there were photos of him and his recently deceased wife on the makeshift altar in one of the gorgeous rooms at the now defunct (big sigh of sadness) East/West Bookstore/Yoga Studios in New York City. To study with him in Ireland for a week cost three grand at the time. Wasn't gonna happen. For $20 and a couple of hours downtown, I was willing to check him out.

I was totally turned off by this evening of prayer, meditation, and social weirdness until, at the end, they played a tape of "himself" ohm-ing in a lyrical, angelic voice. It erased all of the irritation that had been building up within me that evening. Then they played Indian Dude ohm-ing. His voice, too, had a calming effect on me. What was it about the gaze and voice of this man and his teacher?

I was betwixt and between in my assessment of this character. Didn't like the groupies, but was intrigued with his motif (a symbol he "created"). Liked his voice and pretty visage, didn't like the *altar* with said visage (I'm not into people or icon worship—false idols all). Months later, a five hour seminar with the guru in question was offered in New York for $75. Since he was being imported and I didn't have to fly to Ireland, this seemed a steal. A real bargain! I invited others. A few came. Quite a few, actually, and the event itself was packed. Mostly women, I might add. I wasn't the only one to be entranced by his gaze, mystique, "aura," and pretty face.

I sat in the front row, eager to bask in his energy, as was every other gal, also aware of his beloved wife's recent death. He entered the room to applause. He was shorter than I'd imagined and was wearing an iridescent silk *violet* Nehru style tunic. I expected to fall in love/lust/admiration immediately and…didn't. I continued to feel nothing as he proceeded to talk, rant, cajole, joke, curse, and…scream. This man left me utterly cold. The more he talked the more turned off and even angry I became. I couldn't put my finger on it, but I didn't like him. He was full of himself. He insulted Reiki healing (several of my friends there were Reiki healers and Reiki Masters). He told them the only real healing was via his "whatever-whatever" technique. I don't take kindly to anyone telling me it's his way or the highway. How could he of all people, a guru, an alleged "avatar" not honor other modalities of healing? It's like disrespecting someone's religion. I continued to take it in, arms crossed over my chest, eyebrow raised. I looked around. No one else seemed irritated.

I ignored the envelope his people left on each chair, inviting us to donate money to his cause. He jovially said a dollar was fine, even nothing was fine. But then he warned that if we *had* an extra dollar (or twenty or a hundred) and *didn't* donate it, well, this would create bad karma for us. Sounded like a threat to me! He talked about his wife's passing and said that she only departed when he "released her" by touching her crown chakra. How kind of him. Talk about an inflated ego. His was a kiss of death, more like it. This sick woman would have lasted, what, another 100 years if he hadn't given her the crown chakra send-off? The cancer wasn't good enough? It's good to be the king.

He referenced the Tibetan Book of the Dead and the Bardos (the liminal zones we pass through after death) and gave us each a postcard with a Tibetan mandala (a Thangka) printed on it. He's not even a Buddhist. I guess he felt the need for a visual aid and a global reference. "Do you want to hear what it sounds like when you die?" he asked rhetorically. Who's gonna say no? I didn't even know that death *had* a sound. He got close to the microphone and uttered a prolonged scream at the top of his lungs "AAAAAAAAHHHHHHHHH!!!!!!" Good to know that the fear of death tension *eases up* when we cross over. What kind of a crappy belief system is that? It's no better than hellfire and brimstone (but consistent with his false idol worship). Not exactly a feel-good guy, are you, Guru?

Now that he had aurally traumatized us, he promised to give us individual healings at the end to open our sixth chakra (the third eye). Just like when he let his wife out of the can, he'd release our psychic abilities, or boost them, or suppress or kill them, how would we know? He was a psychic can opener. As much as my discomfort was growing during his seminar, I was still curious as all get-out to see what he'd do, what would happen to me if he "did his thing." *Why* was I compelled? A man who had baffled me from the get go, intrigued, then repulsed me. Why was I still clinging? Did I want my $75 worth? Yes! Was I curious to experience the fireworks display at the end? Yes! Was he charismatic? Yes! Vexing. Yes, yes! I waited and waited. As the afternoon wore on his ranting became more offensive, pompous. And dull.

He changed shirts at intermission, emerging in an iridescent silk *cobalt blue* Nehru style tunic this time. Was this a rock concert? He wasn't sweating. It was a gratuitous costume change. It was coming to the end of his five-hour time allotment and he hadn't even started the healings or openings or pokings. My discomfort grew. The dis-ease in my stomach (my gut, my intuition) mounted until I said "enough's enough" and did what no one else did that day. I walked out. There were hundreds of people in the room, a big old conference room in the lower level of some massive hotel in the theatre district of Manhattan. I looked around as I left. Everyone was immobile, gazing at the master. His son, whom he had insulted, if I recall, as having no real skills, no school learning, a drop out, but under papa's brilliant tutelage was now becoming a master carpenter (or something to this effect) stood there in support (or stupefaction) of the man in blue.

I remained angry for days, befuddled for weeks. I inquired of friends who stayed, not wanting to color their report, but simply asking, "What happened? What did you think of him?"

This *five*-hour event elicited no particular responses. "I guess it was good." "It was interesting." "It was okay."

Okay? They devoted nine hours that day to this man, between the extended hours of the seminar (it ran seven instead of the scheduled five) and travel to and fro. I asked, "What happened?"

One young couple offered, "I don't know, but we were really quiet afterwards and didn't talk all the way home."

Sounds like he shut off their throat chakra instead of opening their brow chakra.

I said, "Did you like him?"

"Yeah."

"Did you learn anything?"

"I don't know..."

Glad we're clear on that.

I asked my Reiki Master friend, "What did you think?"

"It was nice."

"You weren't offended by his putting Reiki down?"

"No, I didn't let it bother me."

"Are you going to study his healing modality with one of his people?"

"I don't think so."

No one had anything concrete to say, either pro or con. All were non-committal. One bought some paraphernalia, including a necklace with his "symbol" and the miniature accordion fold-up icon screen (for "E-Z" travel) with pictures of Jesus, Buddha, Mother Theresa, Irish Dude, Indian Dude, and a few other peers. I don't remember exactly who else. Zeus? Rachel Ray?

I was not at peace for weeks afterwards because I couldn't fathom what was so disturbing to me. I hadn't drunk the Kool-Aid, but I had been *misted* with it. I couldn't say definitively that this guy was awful. All I knew was that I was upset. No one had anything conclusive to say about (I mean against) this guy, including me. I just felt ucky.

I queried two medium friends, both of whom I'd invited, and neither of which wasted their $75 or their time on the event. One of them, an older gal who saw his photo and blurted, "Ooh, does he have a brother?" responded to my question, "Do you pick up anything about him psychically?"

She said, "I just knew I wasn't missing anything."

Okay. The other one took her time getting around to answering me (busy gal) but when she did she blew me away. She knew nothing consciously about him.

She was in the front seat of a car as four of us trundled off to a psychic development circle in Connecticut (home of the afore-mentioned medium). She closed her eyes. "Rasputin."

"Oh, God." I said. That was it. He was a Rasputin. A manipulating mesmerizer (nothing against Rasputin, who may have been a great mystic and healer, but he has a creepy reputation to many, including, obviously, me).

She relayed the words, thoughts, and images as they came to her: "Charismatic. Money." (I'll say. All those $20, $75 and $3,000.00s add up, not to mention all those "cash donations" in the envelopes. Anyone paying taxes on that?). "Money *problems*. Problems with the IRS." (Can't be far off after money problems). "Mesmerizing. Took tender loving care of someone, someone who was sick…"

"Yes," I said. "His wife died."

"Younger women…younger women." (Yes, repeated). "Joanna." (*Not* the name she divulged.) "His lover before his wife died. He has a shady past."

He did refer to himself in the third person during the seminar, saying, "This lad of fifteen years stole money from the church box in Ireland." An interesting confession to make to a large group of spiritual followers giving him money.

My friend continued. "A shady past, not murderous, but shady. His spiritual resume is padded. Why am I seeing California?"

Me: "'Cause he'd be perfect there." New York ain't the only town that likes good-looking gurus with silk shirts.

My friend: "Why am I seeing baseball?"

Me: "I have no fricking idea."

And that, ladies and gentlemen, is an A-1 psychic reading. Can I prove any of that stuff? I don't need to. It confirmed my digestive discomfort and quelled my niggling unease. My intuitive barometer—the one where the mercury kept rising and rising and rising as I observed his proceedings—was dead on…Rock…paper…scissors…shyster!

CHAPTER 8

"BATMAN AND JOSE"

November 14, 2011

It was Friday, 11/11/11. For those in the know about ascension energies, this was a portal opening, as was 10/10/10, 9/9/9 and 8/8/8. Up next: 12/12/12, right before the big day 12/21/12. The energies of spirit are ramping UP. We are being prepared for changes on this planet and we can go quietly, or kicking and screaming. Either way, there is no going back to the dark ages we are emerging from. We're leaving misery, survival, and striving behind. Happy days are on the horizon, but first, there is some tidying up to do.

Mother Earth is stretching, creaking, yawning and adjusting her pantyhose as temperatures and water levels rise (be mindful if you own waterfront property). The magnetic field of this planet is waning, portending a potential pole shift and an upcoming (but by no means imminent, Ice Age). Dictators are dying. Markets are withering. Walls, both symbolic and literal, are coming down. With spiritual light growing by the day, what was hidden under a rock is now scrambling, but there's no cover anymore. Check out Patricia Cori's channeled book, *No More Secrets, No More Lies* about the diminishing of the dark energies that have dominated this planet for millennia.

Pedophilia, whether sanctioned by the Vatican or the American Church of Organized Sports is finally being dealt with out in the open. This is a time of reckoning. It is judgment day. Not the end of the World, but *the end of the world as we know it*. A thousand years of peace is on its way, as promised.

We The People are claiming our God-Given Power back. We're crying out, tightening our belts, and going to battle to reclaim our government, our lives, and our planet. It is an exciting time, isn't it? Is it scary? Sure! As with any battle, fighting is how we discover what we're made of. Recall what John Wayne said: "Courage is being scared to death but saddling up anyway."

So put down the Starbucks and do something. Sign a petition. Hug your child. Meditate. Clean your house. Claim your Sovereignty as a Son or Daughter of God. We're not guaranteed anything in this world except breath, death, and taxes. The rest is up to us. We are still a wealthy, wasteful, and unappreciative culture. All the shit coming to the surface needs to be flushed. We are doing it. We are weathering this storm. We are finding each other in the process.

A foursome gathered at my home on Friday 11/11/11. It was a friend's birthday, and I cooked. This is a friend who has not been traditionally comfortable with his own birthday, concerns about aging, I suppose, where he is in life, and what he has to show for himself. I have these concerns too, or had, as they are fading (somewhat).

My spiritual studies lead me to believe that I have nothing to prove to anyone (especially me) to validate my right to exist and, drum roll please, to be happy. I don't need a family or a job to define me. (Yes, this has been my challenge—I am talking to myself.) We rely on these roles as crutches and think that the labels (mom, wife, business owner, maid) are who we are. We also believe they "create" our happiness or unhappiness. "Everything would be great if I was married!" or "Everything would be great if I was divorced!" Clearly, neither marriage nor divorce is the source of our happiness. Our chosen perspectives are.

Happiness is a state of mind I create, irrespective of circumstance. This is the secret to life—to not view "things" we want as the source of our comfort but to our choice of mindset, regardless of what's materializing. We all know the kid just *dying* for a toy who bores of it minutes later. (Here's to Milo in *The Phantom Tollbooth* by Norton Juster, one of my favorite books, now celebrating its 50th anniversary. It's a divine fairy tale for adults, really.) Our highs are fleeting so we look for more "things" to create another temporary high. Voila, our landfill, debt, and divorce problems. Even marriage or a job is a thing. It's what we do with that thing that determines our enjoyment level. Our attitude and perspective comes directly from our choice of thoughts and beliefs. *That* we control. The weather? Not so much.

On this particular day, I cooked and cleaned up a storm in preparation for my friends' arrival. I was donating a loveseat to the birthday boy in anticipation of the arrival of my new one, and my cousin offered to transport this upholstered mound in her van-like car. She figured if it didn't fit inside we could throw it on the roof. My other two friends are strong, so this was the ideal time to feed, fete, and hoist.

I removed the cat and dog hair off my couch as best I could and apologized that the underside had been shredded by my cat Wilbur (now dead). I artfully taped up the bottom with huge sheets of white cardboard and white duct tape so the frayed lining wouldn't hang like fringe.

My cousin arrived after 7 p.m. so that she could park legally on my street. She said, "There were parking cones everywhere except in front of your house. I parked right in front."

"Perfect!" I said.

One by one, all three of my guests rolled in—one from work, one from seeing a movie, one from Long Island. We had some laughs, including a joke by the birthday boy about an oversized superhero hurling deadly sparks generated from between his thunderous thighs. We enjoyed bottles of wine and I gave my cousin her combined Christmas and birthday present early, since I don't see her regularly.

Time rolled by and I suggested we start moving furniture since it was 11 p.m. I had an early morning, and they had a long haul ahead of them getting the loveseat to Queens. Two powerful guys and two capable women took the feet off of the small sofa, removed the pillows, and started shimmying the piece around the corner into the hallway. It wouldn't go past the door. We were stymied. Well, how'd I get it in? It'd been many years since its arrival but I then remembered the delivery guys taking the door off. I ran to get hammer and screwdriver and quickly knocked the pins out from the hinges, hoping neighbors in my apartment building wouldn't be too upset since the pounding was over in seconds. Door off. Loveseat through. Hurdle one.

Out into hallway, onto dolly cart (random aside: sounds like D'Oyly Carte Opera Company, doesn't it? I just love Gilbert and Sullivan), down the elevator, through the basement of the apartment building, and up the ramp to the street. My cousin and I went to her car. She'd gotten a ticket. "Oh, no."

Everything had been going so well. She is not, however, a complainer, so that was that.

The loveseat did not fit in her car. It now had a small tear from the move. It was freezing outside. None of us were wearing coats. The guys shoved it in the car somehow, its padded ass hanging out in the air. They strapped it in and down with twine, knotted firmly by a gay guy who'd never been a boy scout, but by golly, that loveseat was going to Queens! There was talk of my cousin getting another ticket with her back door open and the loveseat hanging precariously over the edge.

I said, "Lightning doesn't strike twice." And then an MBO (most benevolent outcome) prayer (thank you, Tom T. Moore and *The Gentle Way*) for "a most benevolent outcome for my friends to travel safely and easily with no interference, and may the results be better than they could hope or expect!" We were exhausted and shell-shocked from the late hour, food, wine, icy temperature, and heavy lifting. They drove off.

Turns out the cones had been put up because a film was shooting the next day. The signs, which my cousin hadn't noticed, said "CARS LEFT AFTER 10 PM WILL BE TOWED." It was 11:45 p.m. when they shipped out. She was lucky to just get a ticket. The next day I asked my doorman what film was being shot. He is a delightful older man from Puerto Rico, always jovial, almost giddy at times, he's worked in my building for decades and I love him. A jubilant human being, you'd never think he'd worked a day in his life. Jose, happy and energized most of the time, is proof that you can be happy no matter what. Jose is grateful for his job, and the second home he has in Puerto Rico. He seems to relish life and takes joy in providing service. A young Irish American fellow down the street, also a doorman, hates his job with a passion. He blames the job for his misery and claims that no other job is any better.

I told him some people love their work and that he should open his mind to finding something more fun for him. He doesn't believe me and is content to stay where he is, whining, and smoking himself to death. As one psychic said to me, "Some people are happy to be unhappy." That's a lot of people, isn't it?

Anyway, I asked Jose what movie they were shooting and he told me "Batman."

I said, "Who's in it?"

He paused then playfully replied, "ME!" I stopped and thought about it.

"Batman and Jose?"

We laughed.

The birthday boy loves his new loveseat. More to the point, his cats love it. The excavating that my former cat Wilbur so deviously effected was thoroughly appreciated by Bill's several felines who are now living permanently *inside* the piece, sort of like the "mole people" who live in subway tunnels. I am still apologizing to Wilbur's spirit for getting so mad at him when he did the original shredding. Yes, it's all for the best. Eventually.

My cousin isn't stressing about the ticket. She's still thrilled with the handbag I got her for Christmas/her birthday, so she's choosing to focus on the good, not the bad. I am grateful they all got home in one piece, including the loveseat, with no further incident, tickets or tears. We four friends really love each other. We've had ups and downs as friends and cousins, but the convergence by the four of us on 11/11/11 was as remarkable as the day itself.

The portal opening was a portent of the beauty, spiritual energy, and upliftment growing daily on Planet Earth. There have been months and years when various combinations within this fab foursome were not talking to each other. But here we were, older, together, putting our wisdom into practice.

CHAPTER 9

FUCK THE POST

November 19, 2011

I'm not into crowds. I don't like parades. I don't like protests, although I've been to a few animal activist events. The most I'm willing to do is hold up a sign. I don't like the discord that yelling engenders. Most screaming people are vitriolic, and so are the passersby who shout back. God forbid you're wearing leather while protesting the sale of fur (as I have. I am neither vegan nor vegetarian). I'm one of the people who see a big difference between leather and fur, though I don't doubt there are egregious abuses within the leather industry. There are abuses within the dairy and egg industries as well, which is why we should all endeavor to buy organic and humane-certified products, a step in the right direction toward the humane treatment of animals. While I await the day when all animals are treated humanely, at least cows get eaten. Foxes do not. For an animal to be anally electrocuted and skinned alive after a life of incarceration and despair for someone's vanity, I'm afraid there's nothing civilized I can say about that. It's time man stops thinking only of himself and his immediate wants. There's a bigger picture for all of us. Eating fast and cheap food, when you're poor, seems like the only option, but when obesity, diabetes, and heart disease set in, it's obvious that it was a false economy for it created disastrous results of its own. We need to move toward healthier, greener lifestyles as a people on this planet. We are only as strong as our weakest link.

I protested the sale of fur in front of JCrew on Fifth Avenue. It was evening. A fashionable young man exited the store. He looked at me and said, "Valerie?"

"James?" I answered, somewhat sheepishly.

A lovely fashion designer from England, I knew him from my days working for JCrew corporate, downtown. We had a totally pleasant exchange ignoring the fact that I was protesting his company. I pretended I was holding a sandwich, not a sandwich board. JCrew subsequently gave up its usage of fur and many other brave labels are doing the same. If you live in Alaska and eat the seal, please, wear seal fur. If you live on Fifth Avenue and insist that it's the only thing that truly keeps you warm, you're full of crap. Get in your limo and shut your trap. Fur is a status symbol, plain and simple. There are other ways to stay plenty warm.

For vegan absolutists, please note that there is a huge difference between eating an organic egg from a free range chicken and consuming *foie gras*, the product of torture when a goose is forcibly engorged with extra calories, for those of us non-vegans who at least want better lives for the farm animals. For those who love fatty organ meat, put some butter and cream *on* your sautéed liver, buddy, not *in* it while the duck is alive. We all deserve a good death (praise be to Dr. Jack Kevorkian). Most animals in food production are treated deplorably. I believe that revolution is necessary, but that change, ultimately, is incremental with some quantum leaps along the way. Perhaps we will all be vegan someday. Until then, do the best you can, and ensure that the best keeps getting better, for you and the lives of the animals, workers, and land that produce your meals.

For those that wish to agitate for change, more power to them. Radical times require radical efforts. I'm all for the animal liberation front, whose "by any means necessary" (with no harm ever to human or animal life) approach is a-okay by me. They've destroyed property. Boo hoo. The companies affected torture animals. The infiltrated buildings are concentration camps. The victims are rescued. There's nothing like a daring man saving a tender bunny to turn me on.

No one gives a rat's ass about what happens to rats' asses in labs, all so we can wear mascara and drink tea. Seriously, *Nestea* is testing on mice. What could they possibly be looking for—to see if it stains the mice teeth? If humans were subjected to a fraction of what we do to

God's "other creatures" (the "other" white meat) we would be screaming like the guy in Munch's painting. If we had the air or means to scream, which most of those poor animals don't, given the tubes, cages and crates they're shoved in, unable to move, ever. It's unconscionable. This world will be balanced and saved by the feminine love of compassion. It's the Seventh Wave. I read in Barbara Marciniak's channeled book *Bringers of the Dawn* that a time will come when everybody's heart chakras will be activated, as part of the ascension process we are currently undergoing. The men and women involved will suddenly *feel* what their victims (the lab and factory farm animals) are feeling, and they will run screaming, mortified by what they've been doing, never to return. I can't wait.

So, back to protest and the *Post. The New York Post.* I don't buy it. I don't read any paper or magazine except the metaphysical monthly, *The Sedona Journal of Emergence.* My dog pees on the *Times* retrieved from the recycling room in my apartment building, or "The Library" as my senior neighbor Shirley calls it. We share what we find with each other. *People* magazine is a top score. Couldn't pay me to buy it, but it's a cheap thrill from the trash.

I don't like the newspaper because it's dirty. It sullies the hands and the mind with distraction, ads, and bad news. Why read about the destruction of the environment in a paper that contributes to it? Where's the value in so much minutiae? Harvard biologist E.O. Wilson said, "We've got too much information and not enough wisdom." I'd rather be a happy New Yorker than a savvy one. Save a tree. Get your info on the net.

After a beautiful walk in Central Park this morning with my ebullient pooch, I trudged up my ten flights to boost the workout. Did any of you see *No Impact Man*? Great documentary by New Yorker Colin Beavan, who decides to say goodbye (incrementally) to most standard living practices to reduce his carbon footprint. He enlists his wife and their unwitting two-year-old daughter. They even eschew public transportation and walk or use their scooters everywhere. Eventually they phase out electric usage in their home, hooking up a solar panel to the roof of their apartment building so dad can juice up his computer. I mention this because they lived on the 11th or 12th floor, and after giving up their gym membership, lost twenty pounds each within two weeks just by walking upstairs. I'm just saying…

While on my building's concrete "Stairmaster" (I'm on the tenth floor) I hit upon Wednesday's *Post* in the "library" (the stairs are adjacent to the trash rooms). The cover touted the ousting of "Occupy Wall Street" protesters in Zuccotti Park at one in the morning last week. Andrea Peyser's piece, "Sanity Prevails – but Loons Just Don't Get It," bemoaned the filth of the park and referenced the "scum" living there and making it unsanitary. I'm guessing she's a conservative.

I love rabble-rousers. The original Boston Tea Party ranks high. I like WikiLeaks, Julian Assange, Bradley Manning, Valerie Plame, Michael Moore, Tim

DeChristopher, Roseanne Barr, Anita Hill, Norma Rae (a fictional character based on a real person), Sojourner Truth, Harriet Tubman, Karen Silkwood, Susan B. Anthony, *The Blind Side* mom, and anyone who busts an unfair status quo by *taking action*. Passive whiners be damned. Change isn't neat and clean.

The *Post* insults the protesters' tattoos, piercings, personal hygiene, and the state they left the park in. That's offensive? It's *abhorrent* that 55,000 people die *daily* on this planet due to starvation or starvation related illness and that many don't have clean water or sanitation at *all*, let alone fancy public parks that cater to the wealthy. This country gets up in arms when three thousand of their people die in a surprise terrorist attack on a September morning, but most are indifferent to the tens of thousands *elsewhere*, dropping like flies every day because they're indigenous, indigent, riffraff, beggars, workers, savages, pagans, Muslims, or third world. Not our people. Not our problem. We have enough on our mind.

"As above, so below" also means "as over there, so over here." What we do and think affects everybody. You may not see that from an egocentric perspective, but when you open your heart and activate your spiritual vision you will see the filth that lurks beneath the surface of some of the "cleanest" and most "upstanding" of our citizens. Dazzled by shiny objects, we are distracted from the truth. Not all that glitters is gold. I'd hate to see Donald Trump's aura.

Peyser called the protesters "scum." I'll tell you who the real scum are. The executives of Exxon, Chevron, and BP, trying to cover their asses, protect their fortunes and their futures, with no concern whatsoever about the devastation caused by their avarice. The villains are the men that caused the "Savings and Loan Crisis" and the good people (yes, most of them men) of Enron, Halliburton, and Monsanto. People who toe the line only because they have to, not because they give a shit about the water or dead birds or dolphins or other peoples' livelihoods that they've killed. The smelly dope head in Zuccotti Park is a lot cleaner than those guys, let me tell you. It's not only the body that reeks. Souls reek, too.

Don't like Occupy Wall Street? I'm not crazy about this recession. I don't like that banks were given 700 billion (or eleven trillion as I heard, when all was said and done) to enable big bonuses to reward crooked performance during an economy still in the toilet. I don't like that Savings and Loan farms and homes were lost while the one percent feasted on the flesh of the near dead. I don't like that New York City streets are filled with more and more homeless people, young and old, including Dean, one of my locals, who has no feet and sleeps in his socks and a shawl in a wheelchair under the scaffolding of my local FBI. Something is not working. Wealth is not the problem. Callousness is.

"I wish the protesters were more well-spoken," someone said. I haven't interviewed any of them. I'm sure there are a couple of dope-addled doozies down there, whether protesters or hangers on. Heck, we had an addled dope in the White House last round of Bush, and what about that Dan Quayle fellow? Why should I care there are a couple of weirdoes in Zuccotti Park? Keep them out of my White House.

There was a great sign at the occupy protest: "I Don't Mind You Being Rich. I Mind You Buying My Government."

Yes! I say yes to abundance! You don't have to stomp a police boot on peoples' heads to achieve your goal. When my joy upholds your joy, then we've got something. There's enough for everybody. Really. But we'll never know until the dams come down. And the dams are coming down.

The *Post's* Peyser bemoaned foul-smelling riffraff. The people in Ecuador aren't crazy about having no drinking water and the fact that they're dying of cancer due to petroleum toxins left by Chevron, which Chevron refuses to clean up despite a court injunction demanding it. Chevron owes *billions* in reparations to the people of Ecuador (as yet unpaid) but even that doesn't help the babies, sons, daughters, mothers, and husbands who've already died as a direct result of Chevron's brutishness (see the documentary *Crude*. Kudos to Trudie Styler and Sting for putting their money where their mouths are and helping The Rainforest and Her Peoples).

When Tommy Fox, encamped at Zuccotti for 52 days, said he'd been organizing the donation of apartments to protesters so they could sleep inside, Peyser wrote: "for protesters who didn't care to sleep outside" as if they preferred two lumps of sugar in their Wedgwood teacup. "Makes him sound like a member of the dreaded one percent of richest Americans." Please, Peyser. Like Koch, Trump and Bloomberg are hosting *anyone* on their gilded couches (unless they're getting blown by them). Helping protesters find shelter is not the behavior of the one percent. The problem with the one percent is that they help only themselves to the detriment of others, and yes, I am generalizing. There are some amazing wealthy and super wealthy folk who do care and help. I, for one, am a great admirer of Melinda Gates.

Is Occupy Wall Street a perfect protest? Of course not, and so what? Even the American Revolution was disorganized at times. A couple of assholes fought Hitler. We don't question the battle itself. But make no mistake, good people. This is a war. This is a battle for Planet Earth; her integrity, her honor, her ability to exist unfettered without being stripped, raped, pillaged, and poisoned. This is a battle for human rights, a call for *liberté, égalité, fraternité*. This is a time for action.

Until we look beyond our mortal frame and see the world as an extension of ourselves, our child as an extension of ourselves, our cat as our feline self, our environment as the mineral, vegetable, aqueous version of ourselves, we are doomed to failure. It is our smallness of mind that has hobbled our world.

The sidewalk is mine. That is why I do not litter. The subway is mine. That is why I don't leave food, crumbs, or sticky things on the floor or seats. The air is mine. That is why I do not pollute. The animals are all mine. That is why I endeavor to buy humanely-certified animal products, and eat more fruits, vegetables and whole grains to minimize reliance on animal products.

How we conduct our lives on a daily basis has a profound effect on everything around us. Angry people poison the air. I'm not saying if you have a beef not to take care of it. But those who walk around angry *all the time* solve nothing. They create energetic and physical pollution in the body, home, and workplace.

One of the best pieces of spiritual advice I ever got was from Peter Sonnenberg, the trance channel for Orkie: Breathe. Go Slow. Be Gentle. I add to that: be gentle, *first and foremost with yourself.* We cannot give to others what we do not have.

Love yourself. Real, true love. Accept your foibles. Smile at them instead of cursing them. Embrace your inconsistencies; give yourself credit for how hard you try. Let go. Choose to love yourself warts and all, kit and kaboodle. It is *not* selfish. It is the most selfless thing you can do.

Fill your heart with who you are, Love Incarnate. Give yourself the gift of being at peace and feeling good. Breathe. Go slow. Be gentle.

As we become more patient with ourselves, we become more loving towards the world. We begin within then radiate outward.

As we do so we become more understanding of imperfect revolutions, imperfect people, even the one percent, all while advocating for change.

You do not have to be angry to seek change. You just have to take *action*. OM. PEACE. WEAREALLONE.

CHAPTER 10

"THE LAW OF BANANAS"

November 27, 2011

You know about the Law of Attraction. Even though the premise is thousands of years old and as simple as "like attracts like," *The Secret* DVD dramatized the idea so vividly that many, myself included, were newly invigorated by the concept. But just how Jesus-like are you in your ability to manifest loaves, fishes, husbands, or raises? In our "I want it yesterday" and "Instant gratification takes too long" (thank you, Carrie Fisher) culture, what signs can we look for that indicate that we are, at the very least, on the right track in learning how to manifest our desires?

As nice as it would be to manifest via blinking like Barbara Eden in *I Dream of Jeannie*, or twitching your mouth like Samantha in *Bewitched*, there are many factors that determine how Merlin-like you can be. Do you have conflicting beliefs about your ability to be happy and fulfilled? (For instance, you may want to be happy, but don't feel you deserve it.) Conflicts will cancel each other out and you'll be left standing where you were. Are you skeptical about this whole "law of attraction" thing? Skepticism will cut you off at the knees. What mental and emotional operating systems are you running and do your beliefs support your wants? If you really want to be rich but don't have confidence in your ability to manage money (or are afraid of people wanting your money if you get it), you'll be dead in the water. But fear not. Explore with me a little longer…

Maybe you're not *meant* to have a million or even twenty extra bucks this week. We have a "soul purpose" and a part of us (the invisible, wiser part) that knows what's *best* for us, notwithstanding what we think we want. A parent knows not to let a toddler eat a tub of ice cream, despite his screaming for more. We have lessons to learn. We sign soul contracts before birth, establishing the agenda for this lifetime's soul trajectory. Sometimes it's a tough curriculum. At this time of the ascension, most of us are cleaning house big time. If you take care of business, consistently prioritize your happiness and well-being, cleave to what brings you joy, and move away from what does not, magic *will* start to happen. God is Joy and the happier we are, the more we reflect our true selves, Children of Love and Light. "The Law of Bananas" is my way of saying, "As ye sow, so shall ye reap." So plant jellybeans and lollipops and leave the sour pickles for lunch, not your precious Garden of Dreams. Jettison skepticism and cynicism. Where have they gotten you up 'til now?

Take stock of your life. Decide who and what enhances your sparkle. Who or what does not? Get rid of those downers! Seek out supporters! Watch what happens when you eschew those who question your dreams or right to happiness. (They are invariably unhappy people, so don't take it personally, they're just talking to themselves.) Love supports and inflates; it does not tear down and deflate. Many people have a sick and twisted concept of "love". It's up to you to redefine it. Make it work for you. Make sure you are your own best, indefatigable pillar of support, and if you need to buy cheerleading pompoms, *buy them.*

Around Christmas last year I decided to splurge on luxurious soap. I got a whole box of it. No, two. And those soaps came with free soaps since I bought so much soap. I was steeped in soap. I gave some of it away as gifts. And what did people give me for Christmas? Soap. Lots of it. There was liquid soap, boxed soap, and a boxed/basketed soap set. There were bubbles coming out of my ears.

I bought soap and I got more soap, "like coals to Newcastle" as the saying goes. The Law of Attraction is the secular version of "The Lord helps those who help themselves" or rather, "The Lord lathers those who lather themselves." I became a soap magnet.

I've been on a modest budget for a while now. One could pinpoint the loss of the job and health insurance, the subsistence "living" from unemployment checks (now long gone). Oh right, there's a recession! But there were some new non-negotiables as I navigated my future, even as I experienced terrific fear. I applied one aspect of the Law of Attraction: figure out how to feel good. Feeling good attracts good things. This is a simple and profound truth. I didn't know what I was going to do, but I knew what I was *not* going to do—clerical jobs that were soul killing to me. Whatever you're willing to put up with is exactly what you'll get. I wasn't willing to put up with a corporate job again.

I became a fierce advocate of my own happiness. The trick was not falling into the abyss of "OHMYGOD WHATAMIGOINGTODO? What will become of me? What if I lose my home, mind, money, youth, and marbles?" It is a skill, skirting the dark path of "what ifs," and instead choosing medicinal convictions such as, "What if my life is about to become *amazing*?! Better than ever? Happier than ever? Better than I could hope or expect?" Why aren't *those* the "what ifs" that we ponder? Mark Twain said, "I've worried about a lot of things in my life. Most of which never happened." Why do we default to: "Oh God, God help me, I'm fucked?"

I've had many temp jobs over the years (being an artistic type), and regular paychecks being a *useful* thing, many "get by" jobs have turned into "can't live without" jobs (I get excited when I can buy things). But then reality sets in. I'm an indentured servant to a position I find abhorrent. A wage slave trapped in golden handcuffs. Well, aluminum, actually, given my pay.

My last temp job was in a very tense environment (an Ogre boss was to blame). It paid better than many offices in an attempt to retain employees longer than the average twelve minutes new folk generally lasted. There was a lot of waste in this office and a lot of fresh fruit left over Friday afternoons and I took it. I gave it to the bus driver, people on the street, and my neighbor. I even accosted a postal worker with a banana at rush hour. I pointed the fruit toward his abdomen and blurted, "Want a banana?" Profoundly confused, he declined, and scurried away. My colleagues laughed. Nervously.

When I lost this job it was a relief and petrifying all at once. How would I survive? Where would I get my fruit? I heeded Joseph Campbell's call to passion and "followed my bliss." Which meant maintaining my distance from misery. Which meant no more hateful jobs.

That night a friend called to kvell over the success of a writing project. I went into a tailspin. I tried to be happy for her but was unable to despite my attempts at being supportive and mature. I was jealous. "Why her, not me? Am I doomed to failure?" Unable to answer those questions I did something that didn't warrant debate or introspection. I bought some bananas. I went nuts. I bought five.

I did not sleep that night. I listened to every goddamn calming meditation CD I own, real peaceful shit. Usually works for me. Not now. I had a panic attack, a term I use loosely since it wasn't a clinical one. A clinical one is what my Ogre Boss had when I sassed him back one day and he ended up in the E.R. that night. I had responded to his torrent of venom so calmly and succinctly that he was speechless until he fired me.

I arose exhausted from my night of tossing and turning. I was convinced that I would never earn a living at anything creative, that I'm loser, also, that I would die single. Feeling destitute and desperate, I did the only thing a person with no self-esteem could do. I contemplated a clerical job. I'm not knocking it for anyone else, but for me, at that time, it was tantamount to defeat.

Going to the interview felt like the long march toward the executioner. A homeless guy on the subway made eyes at me as I stared ahead hopelessly, stuffed into my suit. Not the sign from God I was looking for. I was prepared to sell myself out for massive amounts of cash, but it turned out the going rate wasn't much at all, and for that, I don't sell my soul. I'm a *high*-priced call girl! But the joke was that this agency knew the Ogre Boss listed on my resume. They had been the very agency sending new employees over every twelve minutes when the Ogre Boss tossed them out the window (after plucking out their eyes). She was amazed I had lasted a year. She told me if I ever wanted to work for 35 cents an hour to give her a call. I grabbed my stay of execution and ran.

My wait for the bus home was long and cold. A chatty grandma chewed my ear off about how much she loved my neon orange purse. It was a briefcase, really, weighed a ton, cost a fortune, and held no more than a sheet of paper, but its color was jaunty proof that I was creative, not "normal." She told me at length about the grandchildren who lived with her and *her* purse collection. Where was the bus?

An old lady pushing a shopping cart stopped and said, "Anybody want some bananas? The fruit guy had extra and I have too many." Since I was well-banana'd back home, I figured someone else would take her up on her offer, perhaps grandma with the hungry grandkids? No one responded.

"I'll take them," I said. She handed me three bananas. While I sat there freezing, I ate one.

Then it hit me...The Law of Bananas. Now I had eight! (Well, seven). It was utterly fantastic. Screw the job, screw anxiety and fear of failure. I was blessed and this was proof. The Universe was giving me cheerful yellow signs to coordinate with my orange bag that everything was okay, that I didn't have to worry, because...well, just because. "Consider the lilies of the field, how they grow; they toil not, neither do they spin." (Of course they don't spin, everybody knows that!)

Then I remembered all the fruit I'd given away while working for the Ogre Boss, the postal worker I'd frightened with my surprise banana assault, the neighbor I'd lavished with grapes, the security men in the Ogre's office building who liked pears and oranges, respectively, and the bus driver who took the apples. This was also the Law of Karma, was it not? She who gives fruit, gets fruit? She who has soap and fruit acquires more of the same. I looked at my life with renewed appreciation of the liberation I'd created. So I was on a budget. I was free.

The next day while out walking my dog (who looks like Snoopy) I picked something up off the ground. It was a small toy from the 1970s, a plastic Snoopy with paw raised, poised over a typewriter. ("It was a dark and stormy night...") It was a sign. From God, the Universe, my Higher Self. I don't care what you call it. Destiny was involved. It was confirmation that I am a writer. It was inspiration for me to write.

Magic unfurled after Snoopy appeared. An editor friend told me to write every day even if I didn't have any obvious trauma to whine about. Another amazing friend suggested I take a writing class and offered to pay for it. One thing led to another and the good vibes began to snowball. I began to see myself differently, as a person who *could* do what she wanted, and *didn't have to* do the things she didn't.

Not long after, I met with a pal and her boyfriend. We talked about life and work, and I said that passion and magic were my guiding principles these days. He countered with rational motifs but I'd have none of it. I shouted, "Passion! Break out of the box! BREAK OUT!" I leapt up to leave. As I put on my coat he offered me a banana. I stood, stunned. He wondered what he'd done wrong. I screamed, "It's a miracle!" and hugged him. "It's a miracle!" I repeated as I jumped up and down like Rumpelstilskin. "It's The Law of Bananas!" I took the banana, proof of the

Universe's perfection, benevolence, sense of humor and Banana-nality.

I bounded joyfully out onto the street. I put on my iPod shuffle and what song came on? "Breakout" by Swing Out Sister. Yes. That is synchronicity, my friends. It is being right with yourself, the world and your Soul's Purpose. I did a little jig on the street as I ate the banana. If I'd had a hat I'd have tossed it up in the air like Mary Tyler Moore. When you prioritize joy, magic happens. And *that* is how you know you are on the right track!

CHAPTER 11

WHAT A REAL MAN DOES

December 5, 2011

I watched the documentary *Buck* recently. As a horse lover and fan of redemption stories, this movie hit on both counts. Buck Brannaman is a gentle giant. I don't know if he's tall, but he's my definition of a real man: strong, skilled, humble, focused, and gentle. Buck is a horse whisperer, some would say "the" horse whisperer, however Buck credits Ray Hunt and Tom Dorrance, the men he learned from, with guiding him. Confident people never take all the credit.

This story is particularly resonant now because it lies in stark contrast to the debacle currently plaguing Penn State. There was a spirited conversation in my home recently between good friends A) a hilarious and opinionated theatre person, and B) an assistant District Attorney in New York. The discussion was about whether a particular individual implicated in the Penn State case was guilty for having witnessed one of the rapes and reported it only to the school authorities and not to the police. According to school policy, the witness followed proper protocol (thereby protecting the school's "good image" but not the child). My theatre friend felt that nothing criminal had been done since the witness, a school employee, did all he was required to do by his employer. My ADA friend, who prosecutes sex crimes, was in vehement opposition.

I said nothing (much) but agreed with my lawyer pal. There's school protocol and there's state law, which was ignored. Then there's that "other law." The Higher Law that comes from a Higher Authority. Not from above. Not from Hebrew National. From Within. Now I know I'm treading terrain that some would consider a slippery slope. This is a subject that is subject to…subjectivity. However some things obviously merit piping up about. Like a lengthy stabbing murder outside one's *low* second floor window (Kitty Genovese, murdered in NYC, 1964, because *none* of her many neighbors who heard her screaming while being stabbed called the police. How do you sleep through an event like that, just swig some Nyquil and put a pillow over your head?) And things like witnessing a child being raped. We all know about the blue wall of silence protecting the police and the unspoken rules, codes, and threats to protect groups or individuals from getting into trouble. But what of those that are hurt? What of the victims of those being protected? You don't want to get your friend, your boss, or your school in trouble, so instead, *more children get raped*. Seem like a fair trade? There's nothing wrong with protecting your own interests, but not at the expense of other peoples' well-being.

Who saw *Internal Affairs*, 1990, directed by Mike Figgis, starring Richard Gere, Andy Garcia and Laurie Metcalf? It's an amazing flick about police corruption, epitomized by Richard Gere, playing Dennis Peck (hardy har har). William Baldwin, his accomplice, gets mortally trapped in Gere's web of evil. There's an extremely chilling moment when Gere is perpetrating some obscenity, smiling about it, and shushing his sideman, Baldwin, with a simple finger to his mouth. Smiling and shushing, simultaneously. Or am I confusing this scene with Christopher Walken and Sean Penn in *At Close Range*, 1986? Yes, I think I am. Oh, well. I'm not editing. *Internal Affairs* deserves the plug for the superior thriller and morality tale that it is. Peck is the creep and Baldwin is his fall guy.

Far from being the end of the world, 2012 is a time of revelation, radical authenticity, and claiming our sovereignty. People are risking their lives the world over to "Fight the Power" (a great song by Public Enemy) to free their lives, their voices, and their countries. It is the quiet voice and the simple act that carries as much weight as the mightiest revolutions. In fact, it is those voices and acts that start and sustain revolutions. The revolution I refer to here is one of healing and of love.

When Buck Brannaman was a little boy, he and his older brother Smokey were professional cowboy ropers. They were on the pro circuit when they were three and six years old, respectively. They executed rope tricks *blind-folded*. They were damn good, and they appeared in a Kellogg's Sugar Pops commercial around 1970, shown in the film (I remembered the commercial from childhood). Buck and his brother were the youngest members of the Rodeo Cowboy Association (RCA).

But their dirty little secret was that their dad was a violent drunk. A violent man. Their mother did her best to protect them but it wasn't possible in full when she was there, or at all when she wasn't. They cringed when Mama went to work as a waitress and they were condemned to an evening alone with their dad, who was merciless in his meanness. Stories like this often go from bad to worse. Their mama got cancer and died when Buck was eleven. The plot thickened. The abuse intensified.

One night Dad got the two boys settled at the kitchen table and started in on the yelling that inevitably led to the beating. As he closed in on them, Buck made a decision that would change his life. He ran out the door. Knowing full well he might be beaten to death when his dad caught him, he couldn't remain complicit in yet another beating by just sitting there waiting for it. He ran out into the dark and found protection and solace (though no warmth) on that freezing night by hiding in the old oil drum that housed their beloved bloodhound, also freezing, in a tiny bit of hay. When Buck came out in the morning and his dad saw him, instead of beating him to death Pa acted like nothing had happened. Buck's life changed that day. Without speaking, he had said, "No."

One day at school the football couch told young Buck to get in the showers with everyone else. He refused. Coach Claverly rode him hard despite the boy's resistance. When he finally got Buck in there, he saw the flesh torn from neck to ankles on the back of the boy's body. Claverly stood there and said simply, "Nah. We'll have none of that." Then he took swift action. Nothing in the school's books told him what to do. This was back in 1970 before child protection laws were in place. He didn't go to the school principal. He went to the Sheriff.

In the middle of the night Deputy Sheriff Johnny France entered the Brannaman residence. He scooped those boys up and as he did he said, "Your dad will never beat you again. I'll make sure of that." I'm sorry he didn't take the poor frozen bloodhound, too.

"We'll have none of that," said one man, and "Your dad will never beat you again. I'll make sure of that," said another as they followed through with their actions. Simple words and few. Do they move you? They sure as hell move me. Because that is the Voice and Hand of God. That is the Divine speaking and acting through Her ambassadors, Holy Coach Claverly, and Sacred Deputy Sheriff France. Men of God. Not because of the church they went to, I have no idea about their religious faith. But because that's what a real man whose heart and mind work together in concert does. He takes bold action. That's what we are all capable of, being Human and Divine simultaneously. In fact that's what we *are*. We are all children of God. How many of us claim our lineage? We're too self-absorbed with the human part to think about the God part. Sort of like siring a child but not raising it. We're half there. Impregnating someone does not make you a parent. Until we claim and act on our divinity, we're just human. There's so, so much more to all of us.

Coach Claverly and Sheriff France saw clearly and more importantly, acted decisively. Contrast that with the bumbling nonsense going on at Penn State today. However many years the Brannaman abuse had been going on, it was resolved within 18 hours when two men, one from scholastic sports, one from the law, took action. The power of Good spoke through Its ambassadors, whose eyes, ears, hearts and minds were open. Like Human Angels, these men made good on their promise to the boys.

Buckshot and Smokey were placed with Forrest and Betsy Shirley, a couple who raised 23 foster boys over the years. More ambassadors. More angels. I told you this was a redemption story. Betsy Shirley said, "They were two frightened little boys but it wasn't too long before they turned into Shirleys. When our kids were little it was like a zoo here, every man for himself and survival of the fittest. My motto that's stood me in good stand is, 'Blessed are the flexible for they shall not get bent out of shape.'"

Buck was terrified of men when he arrived at the Shirleys'. New Dad Forrest walked up to Buck. "He was 6'4" and looked like he was made of rawhide and barbed wire." (Are all cowboys poets?). He shook Buck's hand. Then he went back to his truck. Forrest Shirley huddled in the cab. Buck had no idea what he'd be bringing back, a whip, a shotgun? He returned with a brand new pair of buckskin gloves and handed them to Buck. "You're going to need these." Shirley started Buck on the farm's fence repair work right then and there. Buck said, "I was like a skittish colt, petrified. He understood I just needed something to do."

Buck counsels his own clients now. He runs horse clinics all over the country. "Do you discipline and discourage or do you discipline and encourage? There's a big difference between being firm and being hard." With the power of his wisdom and love, Buck works silent equine miracles in minutes. He demonstrates the difference between *force* and power.

Buck Brannaman and the horsemen he learned from knew the value of gentleness. Having experienced its opposite, and unlike others, he broke the chain of abuse. Buck, his mentors Ray Hunt, Tom Dorrance, Forrest Shirley, Coach Claverly, and Sheriff France are men who knew the strength of tenderness, the power of compassion, the beauty of discipline without disdain. These are real gentlemen. Real men.

Buck is now married and has a lovely teenaged daughter with silky golden hair to below her bottom that looks like nothing so much as a horse's tail. She's a powerful horsewoman, a natural, her father's daughter. Yes, this is a story of love and of healing.

CHAPTER 12

THE GERRY BEAR

December 11, 2011

All right kids, gather round the campfire…It's time for magic. Are you ready? You can fancy yourself logical and well-educated and still make room for the profound and inexplicable. I'm smart enough to know I don't understand everything, but I can feel my way through realms unknown. In other words, I activate my intuition, hone it, and sharpen my skills, so I can discern "other" things from "other" worlds. You know the invisible worlds I'm talking about, right? The signals that transport images from TV station to TV set, from a network studio to your living room, all through the airwaves. The great Canadian philosopher Marshall McLuhan said, "Do I believe in an invisible world? Of course. I watch TV."

Try explaining a digital watch to a peasant in the Middle Ages. Or a microwave oven. An iPhone. All magic is science not yet understood. So suspend disbelief like all smart children and enchantresses do. It is time for Great Things. Time for Salvation, Redemption, Upliftment, and Ascension. The time to lift our eyes up to the Heavens and out of Page Six (tabloid trash talk for New Yorkers).

I'm an unabashed mystic. I know some, perhaps many, of my friends think I'm cuckoo for Cocoa Puffs and that's fine with me. But why is Harry Potter so successful? The Catholic Church? Either everybody is nuts or everybody's onto something, like a dog homing in on a scent. I'm not going to defend the intelligence of people who believe in things they can't see. I, for one, am a firm believer in the Atom, the Microbe, and the Virus.

I've been on a vision quest for a long, long time. Having lost my parents at an early age contributed to that. My parents being spiritualists was another factor. The fact that I have always known that there is more to this life, this Earth, than meets the naked eye, is the capstone. Einstein said, "The more I study the universe, the more I believe in a higher power." He also said, "There are two ways to live: you can live as if nothing is a miracle; you can live as if everything is a miracle."

You can be simultaneously practical and mystical. The best of us are. One foot firmly planted in "reality" (the illusion that we live in) and the other in the "dreamtime," one of many other realities we actively, though not consciously (from this perspective), engage in. A foot in each world, we can be in this world but not of it. We have wild and extravagant experiences each night in our sleep. Some people have dissociative or split personalities. Others have secret lives their families and friends know nothing about. Why is it so hard to comprehend that we have a finger in many pies? Our essence is multi-dimensional and inter-dimensional. You don't have to understand this to contemplate it.

I'm not afraid to speak out now. Being a very private person and a walking contradiction (a shy performer, an introspective speaker), I've got plenty of paradoxes co-existing within. We all do. We're not all of a piece. As I get older I'm more concerned with the truth, *my* truth, than what people think of me. So I'm here to share my tale of magic and miracles, mysticism, intuition, tarot and fairy tales. Settle down and get comfortable…how about joining me in some tea? I'm enjoying a small pot of ginger chai with organic milk. Aaah.

Do you know what apports are? They are the physical manifestation of spiritual energy, i.e., things appearing out of thin air, gifts that emerge from non-physical to physical reality. Some believe a spirit, such as a loved one, has brought the gift, which can have symbolic meaning for the recipient. As Hamlet said: "There are more things in heaven and earth, Horatio, than are dreamt of in your philosophy."

Horatio said, "O day and night, but this is wondrous strange!"

That's right, Horatio. Hold onto your hats, dear readers.

There's yet another angle to this mysterious stuff, to quote Lewis Carroll. "Callooh Callay, Oh Frabjous Day!"

Lighten up, kids! We're here to have fun. Seriously. At the end of the day, when all our galoomphing and galumphing is done, it's time to chillax and get jiggy with the Divine, which is another facet of Us. Joy is sacred, my friends. Joy is sacred. Have fun. I'll help you.

I've heard mention of thousands of seed pearl apports dropping from the ceiling during a channeling, or rose petals falling from thin air. I like this. It appeals to me like the Off-Broadway *Gazillion Bubble Show* does to tourists. Personally, I'd like to be the recipient of a handful of juicy, iridescent yellow diamonds. And you? Parisian chocolate? A nice croissant? Is the idea of something beautiful and magical appearing out of thin air delightful and fun? Or too silly a thought to entertain in your sensible head? Fine, stick with your black coffee, *New York Times*, and tax returns (blcch). Or are you willing to wander back to childhood, a time when possibilities existed, the imagination was queen, and you allowed yourself to play? What do you think Einstein was doing all day? He was playing with himself and giving his imagination free reign. He was intelligent and intuitive. Cat naps were pivotal to many inventors, including Einstein and Thomas Edison who received key information in the dream (i.e. subconscious) state. So much for the left brain. It's fine, it's great. But it's not everything.

And where's that old left brain gotten us so far? War. Lots and lots of war. Pollution. Crap economies and thriving recessions. World-wide poverty and the concomitant unrest. Dictatorships. Tyranny. Secrecy. Conspiracies and faux democracies. Oh, and lots of malls, hydrogenated fats, plastic bags and Styrofoam. Yahoo. It's time to go to the dark side, the dark side of the moon, the shadow side, the subtle world of spirit, and the supraconscious. The night sky filled with sparkling stars. Galaxies and Nebulas aglow with color and light. They exist within all of us. The enchantress, the divine feminine is within, even men. It's time to balance male with female, mind with magic. Care to step on my magic carpet with me now?

I equate magic with miracles, by which I mean real events that are (as yet) inexplicable, such as synchronicities, coincidences, doors opening, and things just "working out." And yes, I credit this phenomenon to an understanding and application of the ages old Law of Attraction and what Abraham-Hicks calls "being in the vortex." It's a good place to be. I will now launch into a description of the ongoing fireworks display of magic in my life.

I was out walking my mini, longhaired, black and white dachshund (who looks like Snoopy, the obsession of my youth) in Central Park. In addition to having three-inch legs, hers are somewhat deformed, which means that she hops rather than walks, *and* at an angle. A British woman commented to her friend as we perambulated, "Look, she runs on a bias!" Mimi looks a bit like a seal flopping across the ice when she is out and about.

It was early spring in New York so it was cold, brown, and gray. There were a couple of patches of grass and stray flowers but no leaves on the trees. But oh, so important, the sun was out in blazes. I saw something lying up ahead at a crossroads. It looked like a stuffed animal. Mimi loves stuffed animals, but I figured it had to be dirty and disgusting. It was lying on the ground, right? Some chocolate covered kid used it as a napkin then dropped it while running off toward balloons and cotton candy. (I was seeing Augustus Gloop from *Charlie and the Chocolate Factory*.) I walked on but changed my mind and doubled back to inspect it. It was a Teddy Bear. He was sitting upright, as if waiting for someone.

He wasn't the cutest Teddy Bear I'd ever seen, but most important, he was clean. He was so brand new his tags were still on. Perhaps this would be a suitable toy for my diminutive German dog after all. I looked around guiltily for a second thinking, "What are the odds that this kid could actually *find* the spot that his bear was dropped?" The Park is 843 acres. Little Augustus is probably meadows away crying his little eyes out. Or perhaps Mrs. Gloop has shoved a hot dog in his mouth and promised him two more bears.

The bear, whose tag read "HAPPY," is a Steiff, and no, not one of the high end Steiffs. I coveted Steiff's tiny stuffed pandas and koalas as a kid at the old FAO Schwartz, to no avail. Too pricey. FAO, where Bergdorf's

Men's store is now, used to be mysterious and dark in the 1960s and 1970s, not like the cheez-ey pink plastic FAO pavilion in the GM building today. This bear was large and probably made in China, unlike the old handcrafted pieces from Germany. Still, I figured it cost at least $30. That's a nice dog toy.

Then all the "magic" started hitting me. Did my father leave it there for me? I lost my dad when I was five years old, and *he* had lost his Teddy Bear in a marital accident. My mother threw out the sawdust filled bear from his childhood in Nuremberg, Germany while cleaning one day. She decided leaking sawdust was sufficient rationale to dispense with it. This did not go over well with my dad. Never come between a man and his Teddy Bear.

Through mediums I'd begun having increased contact with both of my parents and was learning the different ways they communicated with me. I started being able to verify the messages, including electronics turning on by themselves in my apartment. My iPod stereo system eerily turned itself on and played one of my favorite songs from 'shuffle mode' while I was two rooms away. I've had enough such experiences that I accept them as the norm now, as friendly communication from those in spirit that I love, although I'm still at a loss as to what many of the messages mean. My toaster turned on by itself while I was in another room and emitted a loud, high-pitched electronic squeal. I figured it was a communication from spirit but who was it from? What was the message? I screamed out, "What does that mean? I don't speak toaster!" Still, I will look first and foremost for a "logical" explanation as to how something "magically" happened.

But then I accept the gift. My parents exist on a different bandwidth but their consciousness, personalities, and love are still here. They're alive. They're just thinner. As I've uplifted my energies over the years, I've been able to receive theirs. By attuning to the higher frequencies and subtler energies, I've been able to perceive and start to comprehend the gifts of Heaven. It's exhilarating. I've made contact. We have conversations. I accept their tangible gifts (or apports) as well as their messages.

So, Steiff, my dog, and my dad are all German. I decided that Dad was gifting my Gerry dog with a Gerry Bear. I get to use that word because my dad fought in WWII with the US Army Air Corps, and he bombed the hell out of Germany, which he emigrated from with his parents when he was five. I am not a fan of political correctness.

Happy the Gerry Bear sat there waiting for me and my pooch. You can come up with whatever explanation you want. It doesn't matter to me. The dawning realization that it was a gift from Heaven grew stronger and stronger. The bear is as big as my dog, and when I was a wee thing Dad gave *me* a doll as big as I was. I don't remember it, that's how small I was. But I've seen pictures of it standing next to me. I look extremely wary of the monstrous mannequin. What was happening now was magic indeed! And to the naysayers I advise they eat a cookie, dance a jig, and *lighten up*. That's how we heal the world. And that's our job, isn't it? The most important directive of the Law of Attraction is to *feel good*. So feel good, good people. Have some fun. Happy people are nice people.

The magic continues. While walking home from Bed Bath & Beyond one day I found a pair of aviator sunglasses on the ground. Now, I wouldn't be caught dead with them today because they're disgustingly *trendy*, however, I sported them as a kid in the '70s and rightfully so, since my papa was an aviator. But for free, I figured I'd take 'em home. I washed them and tried them on. They were men's, way too big for me, so I slated them for my Salvation Army donation bag. I put them on the kitchen counter to dry and froze in my tracks. I was transported in time to the '60s, when my father's actual aviators lay on the kitchen counter, or the dining room table, or wherever the hell they were. I remembered the real horn thingies (that rested on the bridge of the nose) of Dad's shades. (I tried Googling the name of that eyewear element, no easy answer came. Anyone? Like it's important). The hair stood up on my body. My father was in my house. In my kitchen. In my life. It had been awhile since I'd seen his things lying casually around the house.

A few weeks later I found a book in approximately the same spot on the street. It was Randy Pausch's *The Last Lecture* and if you haven't read it yet, do, or Google his actual speech on the Web. Randy was a dashing and brilliant computer science professor at Carnegie Mellon. He was also a devoted husband and father, as was mine. Randy got pancreatic cancer, the same number that took down

Steve Jobs and my mother. So I was on familiar terrain as I read about his descent into illness, and the world of tearing yourself away slowly and consciously from those you love.

The book grew on me as I read it. I got to the part where he spoke to his children so they would know someday (since they were very small when he died) *how* he loved them, *how* he perceived them, *how* he thought of them, it hit me: my father was communicating his love to me through this book. He never got to tell me when I was a teenager, a young adult, an adult, heck, even a *six* year old, how much he loved me, though I got my fill through age five. The guy was a great dad and I remember him clearly. I got choked up. The book was left for me in the same place he left the aviators.

I shared this incident with my friend Bill, a sympathizer on many accounts. Dead parents for one. Sensitivity to spirit, two. Sense of humor and theatricality, three. I recounted my epiphany but remained baffled. "*Why* on earth at Bed Bath & Beyond? What could that possibly mean?"

He said, "Easy. It's from the BEYOND."

That warranted a laugh. He was right, of course. It made perfect sense. The pieces all fit. The brown shades currently rest on the brown book on my opaque pale aqua glass coffee table. It's like having my dad's pipe out. I can practically see the smoke curling up in the air…

So I will conclude with one more short story. Though there are myriad more, there's lots of time to tell all those stories, and I will. A friend called me this afternoon. He is an actor. A playwright. A producer. And an attorney trained at Yale Law. He said, "I thought you'd appreciate this story…I'm due to have a medical procedure next week and in order to have it I have to stop one of my meds…I already forgot once and had to reschedule the procedure because I had taken the contraindicated meds. Well, I was about to take all my meds, including the one I'm *not* supposed to, the pills were in the palm of my hand, and the one I'm *not* supposed to take popped out of my hand and onto the floor of the bathroom."

"Like a Mexican jumping bean?" I queried.

"Yes," he said. "What do you think?"

He knew what I thought which is why he called me. He knew I would confirm what he already knew, which was that something "abby-normal" had happened. His daughter figured his dead mother had done the deed. I said, "Who the hell knows who it was. If it was your mother, she's obviously not ready to hang out with you yet. But it was definitely someone. Coulda' been your guardian angel. Fun!"

So, if you feel an unexplained breeze on your cheek, a cold spot in the room, or you unexpectedly think of someone or something that has some resonance for you when something synchronistic happens, remember, the veil between the worlds is thinner than you think, and it's getting thinner daily with the 2012 energies accelerating. Love never dies. The means of communication changes and we acclimate to those subtleties, like getting used to an iPhone after using Dixie cups attached with string. It's different, but it can be done. And if you're open to those gifts from spirit? Well, let's just say, there are lots of Teddy Bears waiting to be found.

CHAPTER 13

A TALE OF TWO SOLDIERS

December 15, 2011

We live in a world of appearances. This world has been referred to as a school, an illusion or a dream by many spiritual traditions. It's a convincing illusion, as are dreams, hence the comparison. Nightmares are very unsettling while we're in them, sometimes even after we wake up. Similarly, we buy our life story hook line and sinker until we "awake" or die, whichever comes first. And that's how it's meant to be. We're meant to buy the conceit of who we appear to be this spin on the human merry-go-round. We suspend our disbelief for a lifetime. Then we wake up like Dorothy back in Kansas at the end of *The Wizard of Oz*. Did we learn as much as she did? Keep open to the lessons and gifts that life presents to you.

If it's all a dream, then nobody *actually* gets hurt, just like moviegoers who pay to be scared. We *like* to be on the rollercoaster! If everything was hunky dory every day of our lives we'd be bored stiff. That's why we play games and solve problems. We like, no we *need*, a challenge, like a dog needs to chomp on bones. We will never understand the complete bigger picture, but I'm awfully fond of contemplating it. This is a quantum universe. Don't get lost in your Starbucks.

We believe we are this outfit, body, ego, personality, and our accomplishments. When we die we don't take any of that with us. The only thing that comes with us in our heavenly suitcase is the love we gave, the love we received (this is a gift to the giver, as well as to ourselves), and our lessons learned. Life is consciousness. Life/Love/God is ever expanding. And the vehicle of that expansion is us. We the People. You and Me. We are God's Ambassadors, Gods In Training. We increase Her splendor through our experience, we are His field reporters. It uses our eyes to see. We are the hands and feet of the Divine. It's a great job. Contemplate the magnificence of Who You Are.

I love people who step up to the plate, take the heat, rabble rouse, incite the ire of others, sometimes die for it, sometimes not, but always leave the world a changed place. I love Tallulah Bankhead for cartwheeling across the stage with no underwear on and Mae West for saucily bucking the prudish mores of her time. I admire courageous people and intrepid souls who challenge the status quo. My father was one of those people and so was my mother. They helped people anonymously and friend to friend. My mother told me it was always better to give directly to a person than to an organization, because you knew where all your money was going. Many organizations rustle up money just to sustain themselves, with a pittance going to their alleged "cause."

There *are* truly great organizations these days (Greenpeace, NRDC, Sea Shepherd, and PETA for starters) and I donate to them when I'm able. The trend of reaching out to help our fellow man, fellow creatures, and the planet upon which we live will continue as humans wake up to their divine potential and reverse the ill effects of their behavior over the millennia. However, lots of organizations are not as effective as they'd like to seem. The American Cancer Institute (the best endowed charity in the world) comes to mind. Are they in the business of improving things (cancer rates have gone up) or simply fund-raising to feed the machine maintaining their existence? Watch the movie *Food Matters*, chock full of information about health, healing, and the medical and drug industries and decide for yourself.

Personally, I don't believe in any medical research that involves the use and abuse of animals. George Bernard Shaw, the great playwright, vegetarian, and Theosophist said, "Vivisection is a social evil because if it advances human knowledge, it does so at the expense of human character." We are *not* more important than other species on this planet. Earth is one giant organism. The human bone is connected to the bunny bone is connected to the tree bone is connected to the sky bone.

The issue I choose to tackle now is that of appearance, impeccability, and contradiction (yeah, you could call it hypocrisy) within the individual. Since I value authenticity and integrity in my friends and role models, I share these stories with you.

There was a man whose story I was particularly drawn to, one who'd made a name for himself in the 1970s and who shall remain nameless until he croaks. I was moved to tears by the A&E biography about him. His was an uphill battle to do what he believed in, and people reviled him for it. I thought he was impressive, noble, cool, and attractive for an old guy. He had a couple of decades on me.

As fate would have it I met this maverick while traveling. We hit it off right away. It was surreal, meeting and connecting with him. He was odd, garrulous, a bit preoccupied with himself, but the excitement of being with him overshadowed all that. Mostly. I was wary but intrigued. We ended up having a relationship once I got over my qualms about being physically intimate with someone whose body had so much more mileage on it than mine. I also had to contend with the fact that he was loopy and difficult, but I was still clinging to The Legend.

The relationship was difficult. He was impossible to pin down or make plans with. He was elusive. He didn't want to have real conversations or listen to me. When it came down to it, I was only useful to him to the extent that

I gave "good audience" when he ranted his paranoid perceptions while up on his soapbox. When I wasn't pissed, I felt empathy and tried to lighten his load and tickle him into happiness. Instead, his anger and malevolence dragged me down. I took it until his callousness turned to cruelty. He was unbearable. And I was broken. The man who earned his reputation as a person of integrity turned out to be a miserable misanthrope.

The very nobility that I thought he stood for was nowhere evident in his personal life, down to his spitting gum on the sidewalk, a particularly perfidious expression of contempt for his fellow man. He took care of me at times and at others I felt like one of Blue Beard's wives under lock and key. The man I thought of as a model citizen refused to help people in need in his small town. He still has fans that think he's a stand-up guy. They haven't dated him. At his advanced age he's still cashing in on his cachet as an infamous martyr of sorts. Having been through the mill with him, I now think he's just a cranky old man. And I don't believe the gauntlet he ran "made" him that way as many suggest. I think his difficult and selfish nature led him to take on that gauntlet in order to get noticed. From my post-dating perception it was ego, not nobility that gave him the chutzpah to do what he did. It took a self-aggrandizing narcissist to buck the odds and win. Whatever his motivations, he got a tough job done and changed history. He was soldier number one. Korea.

Soldier number two was Vietnam, a man I met shortly after dating Korea. He was new to the storytelling circuit I was already on and he asked for my feedback and advice since I was a seasoned thespian and solo artist. He was my loyal audience member when I performed, and I was his. A former fireman who had survived the 1970s when "the Bronx was burning," his stories were heartfelt and gut-wrenching. He got choked up talking and I got choked up listening. Now, here was a real man of honor. He'd been an EMT medic as well as fireman and shared gruesome tales of life and death, loss and salvation, fear and courage. I was proud to know him. He was grateful to know me, and we shared war stories, mine of dating, his of fires and killing fields.

As time wore on our relationship shifted. He became a big star on the storytelling circuit, New York being hero hungry, particularly for firemen and cops post 9/11. He went from being green to a pro in no time. And deservedly so. He had the goods. Despite my confidence in my storytelling abilities, the organization we performed with elevated him to star status while I got left in the dust. Sigh...

But we maintained our friendship. He was married with kids and grandkids. During a storytelling evening where the topic was intimacy (read "sex") another side of him came out I wasn't so comfortable with. Turns out his marriage had some issues. And the way he expressed those issues was rather disturbing to me: macabre, disrespectful to his wife, and emotionally violent.

Then it turned out he had major issues with one of his children. He wasn't even talking to her. His fury was so intense he said, "If she was lying on the ground dying in front of me, I wouldn't lift a finger to help her."

Gulp. My opinion of him was starting to shift. During other talks, his violent hatred of Barack (seemed his other firemen buddies felt the same way), his opposition to abortion (even though he supported his wife when *she* got one), was giving me pause as to whom, exactly, this "hero" was.

He assumed because my father was a pilot and navigator in WWII and I was proud of him, that I was totally and unabashedly pro-military. Uh, that would be a *no*. There hasn't been a war since WWII that I've understood or approved of even a little. I don't like the loss of civil liberties and privacy we've incurred since ceding our power to our "fear happy" government post 9/11. I don't believe that living in fear and building wall after wall and arsenal after arsenal is the American way, or the answer. The Military Industrial Complex is happy to keep terror alerts alive and their budgets sky high. When people are afraid, they are weak and when angry, blind. Contrary to what most of us think anger is not a *statement* of power. It is a *request* for power. Think about that. Why do animals get all puffed up before a fight? To appear bigger. Same with railing and ranting and waving guns in the air for us two-leggeds. Turns out this hero friend of mine was a very angry man.

He ended up getting a job in the airline industry, which thrilled him to no end. He got to be around airplanes. He was like a little kid going to work, and he was able to travel.

He offered to take me to the Smithsonian Air Museum in Virginia. I wasn't really eager to spend a whole day with him (he assured me it could be done, quick flights down and back), but it was better than his offer to take me to Aruba, which I couldn't quite fathom. He never made a pass at me, and I knew his wife and kids, but the invite wasn't inviting. However, he got me with the aeronautics/Dad angle.

I agreed to join him on a freezing January day a few years ago. He picked me up in his car long before the crack of dawn and launched in on his first tirade about "fucking Al Gore and his fucking global warming lie, it's fucking 40 degrees below zero, there's no global warming..." He was so hot under the collar that he was global-warming the car. I, however, was chilled to the bone by his diatribe. Was I ever in for a ride. As the day progressed he showed me off to his colleagues at the airport. (I was a pilot's daughter, and Dad was an officer at that). I became increasingly uncomfortable. I said less and less as I observed the behavior of, essentially, Major "King Kong" (Slim Pickins) in *Dr. Strangelove*. I was wondering how I would get through this day and rued my decision to join him.

We got on the plane and he remained giddy with joy at the prospect of A) flying, B) going to the Air and Space Museum again (he'd already been several times), and C) it was becoming increasingly clear, being with me. My "sensitivity" was kicking in and I felt his "energy" creeping over to my side of the armrest. I felt sick emotionally, like Penelope Pussycat, the black and white Looney Tunes cartoon kitty that cartoon skunk Pepe le Pew stalks. The day ahead was looking interminably long.

Our flight was delayed because the water in the aircraft's bathroom was frozen. Seemed a petty enough problem to me, but turns out it was major. My companion said we might have to take another flight down south (making the day even longer) or, we could go somewhere else. Somewhere else? I wanted to go home.

I kept quiet and stared out the window. It was a gorgeous day, sunny, clear blue skies, with lovely, puffy white clouds. Frozen with discomfort, I mentally reached out to my dad. "Help," I gulped silently. I desperately wanted to get away from this man. This "hero," too, had turned into a nightmare.

Our flight was cancelled, and when my friend looked up at the flight board to see where else we might go, I looked down at my feet. I was uncomfortable beyond measure and held my breath. Nothing worked out. I couldn't look too excited, but I silently heaved a *huge* sigh of relief. I was too traumatized to be excited, anyway. He drove me back to the city and asked if I wanted to get breakfast. I was dying to get out of his car and away from him.

"No, thanks. I'm not hungry, just really tired." In truth I was *exhausted*. From the cold, from being up at an ungodly hour, and from being with this ungodly man. I said thank you and goodbye and drank two glasses of white wine as soon as I got upstairs before I passed out.

I am learning to get to know people personally and not buy their hype without affirming it for myself. It's important to squeeze the Charmin. The more "heroes" I find have clay feet, the more impressed I am with me. And that's a lesson I want to be learning. The men and women who do the real brave, loving, and honorable stuff are never the folk who blow their own horn, or encourage others to toot on their behalf. Why do we worship folk, anyway? We should endeavor to be the best, happiest, most honorable, and loving people every day. Living our lives, not constantly looking around to see what others are doing. Be the change you want to see, right?

Oh, and one more thing. I (of course) believe that my daddy helped ground the plane. You should know that about me by now. Sure, it was cold that day. But plenty of other planes got off the ground. Just not mine.

CHAPTER 14

THE WOMAN WITH BUBBLES ON HER KNEE

December 18, 2011

She had a brisk walk and an upright posture. A slender woman with New York panache and white hair, she looked to be around sixty or older. I saw her glance at my goofy dachshund and smile gently, and I felt inspired to engage with this woman. I noticed her unique, modern necklace—a string of large, clear-glass bubbles around the size of round plums. Although transparent, the necklace made a strong visual statement. She wore red and grey, the grey tweed skirt offsetting her red sweater so that the color popped. The red further showcased the clear bubbles that lay in a ring around her neck, like she just stepped out of a bubble bath of glass orbs.

She admired my dog. I complimented her necklace. "Thank you," she said. "I just love bubbles."

I paused then launched in. "Do you know what they mean?" I put myself out there as I often do, this time with a stranger.

"No," she replied, but you could tell she was intrigued. I was about to explain her obsession.

I told her about an experience I had at a shamanistic workshop decades ago. Hundreds of us had gone into deep meditation with Lynn Andrews, a teacher whose books I adore. I had been very trepidatious about taking this seminar. Lynn had been through all sorts of tests with her two teachers, Native Americans from Manitoba, Canada. During Lynn's trials with her teachers, she'd been starved, frozen, bloodied, and terrified in addition to being nurtured and enlightened. She was apprentice to Agnes Whistling Elk and Ruby Plenty Chiefs over several decades and became a woman of power herself. What trials and tribulations would she subject us to over the weekend? I wasn't in the mood to eat witchetty grubs (which Lynn did when she spent time with Australian Aborigines).

When I arrived on West 34th Street there were Native Americans protesting Lynn's presence. This added to my anxiety about taking my first ever New Age weekend seminar. The protesters held signs and chanted, "She doesn't represent us!"

Our teacher took to the podium right off the bat inside the ballroom where we were to spend the weekend together. Lynn, a blonde woman from Beverly Hills, spoke calmly and coolly. "The protesters outside are correct. I don't represent them. I represent myself alone, and present to you the tenets of my teachers, Agnes Whistling Elk, Ruby Plenty Chiefs and the Sisterhood of the Shields to which we belong. That is all I have ever claimed." She cut their argument off at the knees. She kicked ass. I was impressed. And relieved.

But I was in no mood to be tested or taunted. This was the Manhattan Center, built in 1906 by Oscar Hammerstein to house operatic and other theatrical events, then purchased in 1922 by the Masons, and is now in the hands of the Unification Church, yes, the Moonies. And this was decades before the sweat lodge "spiritual warrior camp" debacle overseen by James Arthur Ray in Arizona, in 2009, that resulted in the death of three people. At any rate, I had heard of personal growth events where you couldn't go to the bathroom or eat (that would be EST, I believe). I'm big on going to the bathroom and eating. I consider them basic privileges. I'll even go so far as to call them favorite pastimes. I do not like being deprived, and I do not like being told what to do. I thoroughly queried the organizers before signing up. They said I could bring lunch and snacks and that I would have unlimited access to toilets. I continued my interrogation. "We're sitting on the floor? Can I bring a pillow?" I'm no ascetic. I want my ass padded.

"Yes."

They were okay with me being comfortable. Phew! But I was still worried about this mysterious realm I was entering. It wasn't the Australian Outback, but what was it? My inner control freak was having a conniption.

We did many meditations. The lighting was subdued and the ballroom, which was dark and decorated with Egyptian motifs, had a Masonic feel to it. I was reminded of the secret ceremony scene in *When Peggy Sue Got Married*. We delved into the mystical realms of our own subconscious to divine things including what our power animals were. There was live drumming and trance-inducing music. I was in the right place.

As an amusing aside, there was but one man there, and a famous one at that. He must have been petrified to be surrounded by so many women, especially after the recent success of his movie, *Desperately Seeking Susan*. It was Aidan Quinn, wearing an oversized button down navy/green plaid flannel shirt, a wedding ring, and a name-tag that read: "BRIAN." He ascended the stairs as I descended. I looked him in the eye, glanced at his nametag, and moved on. No one else seemed to recognize him. We were there for Lynn, LYNN! We Bacchantes were frenzied in our devotion to spirit and personal growth, not some gorgeous, charming, desirable movie star. I think "Brian" may have been a little surprised and disappointed after all was said and done that no one noticed. Maybe he was relieved. And maybe he had as meaningful a time there as I did.

I was in a happy daze from the dim light, drumming, Lynn's mellifluous voice, the soft carpeting, and my security pillow. But I still had my wits about me, not to mention my emergency snacks (in case I got stranded in the Outback of the enormous Manhattan Center). I purchased an arrowhead carved out of black obsidian meant to deflect and remove negativity and a small abalone shell to hold the sacred sage that Lynn suggested we burn at home to purge the air and welcome Spirit.

I awoke from one meditation lying flat on my back, facing the ceiling (which was very high, this being a ballroom and all) just under the edge of the mezzanine. I could see the room around me: the omnipresent Egyptian motifs, the ornate plaster columns, the hundreds of people (excuse me, women) lying on either side of me. I could see Lynn on the stage and her drummers scattered about the room. I saw something else, too. Approximately six to eight feet above me at about eleven o'clock, there was a bubble. A clear bubble. It was about 18-24 inches in diameter. It looked like a perfect soap bubble except it was not iridescent, and it was unwavering.

I was curious and confused. I knew it wasn't normal. It was extraordinary. So I continued looking around the room to review all the details I just described, saw them clear as day, and the bubble, too. I knew the bubble couldn't "be there" in 3-D so what the heck was it? I put my hand in front of my face. Yup. That was my hand. I even pinched myself like people do in movies. I'd never done that before, but it's what you do when you want to make sure you're not "seeing things," right? The bubble remained. Still lying on my back I twisted my head to the right, eyed the woman directly next to me, glanced at Lynn up on stage, then whipped my head back quickly to see, yes, again, the bubble. It remained fixed in the air six to eight feet above me at approximately eleven o'clock. What rational, material explanation could there possibly be for something like this? There was none. After what felt like ten minutes, the bubble was no longer visible.

I spent the next five to ten years asking anyone "way out" or spiritual, "Do you know what bubbles are? Have you ever seen a bubble?! Do you know what they mean?" Nothing. Niente. I was on my own. But I continued to see them on occasion when I'd awaken from sleep in the wee hours and I was "between the worlds." My eyes acclimated to my bedroom in the dead of night, to the shadows, the nightstand, the light from First Avenue, New York City, all to the soundtrack of the ever-present din of 59th Street Bridge traffic. I was coming to, coming into consciousness, and there would be a bubble, usually to my left, four to six feet above me (my ceilings are not as high as the ballroom), same general size, one to two feet in diameter. Clear, unwavering, inexplicable. One time it glowed red. That seemed ominous. What the heck did red mean? I had no more explanation for the color than for the bubble itself. But by now, bubbles were the norm for me.

Years later I was watching an A&E (or some such) show on Civil War hauntings, about the many historic sites that have unaccountable goings on. Unaccountable, that is unless you believe in ghosts. The battlefields, museums, and historic landmarks all have paranormal activity. They called in a psychic or two to explain what was baffling the staff and guests at one such site. They showed a civil war soldier walking along, presumably a ghost (yes, this was a dramatization). He was surrounded by hundreds of small bubbles. BUBBLES. I was sitting on my couch. I screamed, "BUBBLES! BUBBLES! IT'S THE BUBBLES!!!! BUBBLES!!!" I scared the hell out of my two cats and they shot off. I was on the edge of my seat, glued to the TV. My potential salvation was imminent. "Please, *please*, psychic lady, tell me what the bubbles ARE."

Psychic Lady said, "There are a lot of spirits here."

"SPIRITS!!!!!THE BUBBLES ARE SPIRITS!!!!!" I danced around my living room, whoopin' and hollerin' like a revivalist. I was so gratified that someone could validate, mention, describe, no less SHOW what I had seen. Thank you, Psychic Lady on A&E!

So back to the classy lady on the sidewalk. Sweet. Sad. Overly attached to her dead dachshund, whose (scant) ashes she wore in a tiny charm on her sterling silver bracelet. She thrust her dead dog's memorial card at me. This gal had just inherited a big dog and moved down to New Orleans to give it the space she felt it deserved. She's living in a flood zone. Seriously, people. Coastal living, not the way to go. Katrina was a warning...Don't rebuild in hurricane, flood, or tornado country. Mother Nature will always win. Move upland. The water levels are rising with global warming and will continue to do so.

She was tall, slender, elegant, and could have graced the cover of Town and Country. Her mother had been a show room model in the fifties. Since I'm an avid yakker regarding Spirit and we both love animals, we exchanged emails. She was wearing a pencil skirt and had a tattoo on her knee. I saw it clearly when she bent down to pet my dog. Not what I'd expect for a woman of her ilk. The tattoo was a bunch of multi-colored balloons. All right, so not exactly bubbles, but a similar motif. She was drawn to bubbles and balloons for "gaiety." And yet as I got to know her, I discovered how deeply devoted she was to sadness, grief, and mourning. The tattoo and necklace were vain attempts to cheer herself up.

As we explored friendship, I encouraged her to lighten up, take a *bubble* bath, chew some *bubble* gum, for God's sake. She said bubble baths were indulgent.

"That's the *point*." I replied. "Indulge yourself. You're too serious. You're too sad. Lighten up, have fun!" She had Germanic and Scottish ancestry and wasn't fighting it.

Her middle name meant "sorrow." I knew a girl with the same sad name. She was born as her young father was having a stroke, from which he never recovered. Mother and father were in the hospital at the same time, one giving life, one departing from it. I told Bubble Lady to jettison her sad middle name. She was appalled. She not only LOVED her name but its meaning as well. In fact she was in love with sorrow. Grief was her way to cling to those she loved who'd left the physical.

I've grappled with grief and sadness for many long years. I've also sought to release them, and never with a drug beyond a glass of wine. It's not inevitable that we succumb to our circumstances. We're the ones who decide how we *respond* to the circumstances, and what we believe about them. Was it a tragedy? Or was it an experience? I guarantee if you choose to view something (even something that was terribly hard for you) as a tragedy instead of an "event," you will make it much, much harder for yourself. If your beliefs (say, "life's a bitch and then you die") are not producing happy results, consider some new beliefs if you want to be happier. Take inventory of the software in your head. You're the programmer. A tattoo can't override that.

So, what's in a name? I knew a gal given a *cheerful* name at birth. One of the most depressing people I've met. Just this side of anorexic, smoked, and exercised like a fiend. A New York City classic clad in black, stuck in spin class, sipping black coffee, and pondering morbidity. Turns out she was named to compensate for the death (prior to her birth) of an elder sibling whom she "replaced." I have no reason to believe anyone in her family is any happier than she. Addicted to sadness, misery and grief is a crappy way to go through life. A happy name is no antidote to a sour outlook. In her case, it was false advertising.

So, what's in a name? Whether it's bubbles or balloons, sadness or gaiety, whatever is encapsulated in a name, necklace, or tattoo, there's nothing to a symbol unless you live up to it. Consider Mafioso who wear Christian crosses while they wack people, or $20 handbags sporting the

Chanel logo. "Coco Canal" my cousin calls them (they're sold on Canal Street in Chinatown). Don't talk about it. Be about it.

CHAPTER 15

"SO YOU THINK YOU CAN DANCE, JESUS AND MARY?"

December 29, 2011

As a spiritual adventurer, I rely on my internal GPS to decide what's real, what's not, what has merit, and what has merit even *if* there's some non-meritorious crap attached to it, while I wend my way through the strange, inexplicable, macabre, bizarre, outlandish, and absurd. Like a diamond covered in dirt, you don't toss it because it's soiled, do you? You know a diamond's intrinsic worth despite surrounding detritus. Perhaps it hasn't even been cut yet, and it looks like a murky piece of glass. You clear the dirt. You cut the diamond. You take the gift.

It's easy to dismiss the good with the bad when we judge or write people off. As soon as we discover someone has a human failing, some hypocrisy, a skeleton in the closet, we often dismiss the person out of hand. It concerns me when people don't walk their talk. However, we are all learning, and none of us are perfect (as if you could even define that one). As we teach others, we teach ourselves.

We are flawed, as are most diamonds. Jesus was *human*. And divine, as we are. It's our humanness that makes our ascent in awareness all the more meaningful. Gandhi, human. Martin Luther King, human, JFK, RFK, human, human, *and* exceptional in what they accomplished on this earth. Every saint was a sinner (Saint Francis is a classic example) and every sinner is a future saint. No one is as good (or as bad) as you think they are.

Neighbors defended O.J. because he "seemed so nice." He just didn't want to kill *them*, that's all. He was rich, famous, handsome, and an American football icon, enough to "deify" any person in our culture and blind fans to the truth. The fact that he made Hertz commercials doesn't mean he wasn't homicidal. The best con men succeed because of their ability to blend, assuage, and inspire, before they suck you into their cult, web of lies, or car (like good looking serial killer Ted Bundy). Fault our reliance on veneers, our admiration for a great set of teeth rather than a great character. Our bad.

When the East West Bookshop (may it rest in peace) opened their exquisite yoga studio on Fifth Avenue, NYC, they hosted a bevy of wonderful events, some sublime, and some ridiculous. The classes were affordable at $5 to $25. I heard musician Laraaji (who teamed with Brian Eno in the '80s, among other accomplishments) give a demo on crystal singing bowls, and then I stayed for his concert after. We lay on our backs in the beautiful studio with high ceilings, white walls, blond bamboo floors, soft halogen lights, and white candles. It was a sacred space. He walked among us and played gongs, bells, and chimes over our heads. It was a play space for New Age grownups. This is an example of one of their uplifting events.

Nancy Burson also hosted a workshop at East West. I had seen her years ago at another New Age event I was brought to by Sean David Morton, a New Age speaker with whom I once studied what he called "spiritual remote viewing." I had an extraordinary experience studying "real" CRV (coordinate remote viewing) with former Army Ranger David Morehouse at the Omega Institute for five long days. Being a former military man now friends with Deepak Chopra, he was working (hard) on maintaining his smile and peaceful demeanor, but still ran our class like boot camp. Long hours, intense training, and he did not suffer fools gladly. That week requires an essay all to itself.

Because I was taken with the world of remote viewing (I recommend David Morehouse's book *Psychic Warrior*) I considered doing the (relatively) cheap day with Sean David Morton at New York's classically cheesy "New Age Expo" (or is it New Life Expo? Yes, it is). The place was brimming with purple people and wind catchers, crystals and yoga mats, juicers and fortune-tellers. The cheese factor was high. That does not mean that there were not genuine "gems" amidst the kitsch.

My day with Sean David Morton was exhilarating. Even though we were in a gross conference room in the slightly grizzled New Yorker Hotel on 34th and 8th Avenue. (Lots of spiritual events take place there, and at the Manhattan Center right around the corner). This is the hotel that Nikola Tesla lived and died in. What better pedigree for a space hosting a crowd cleansing and photographing auras? Morton led us through yogic mudras, chants, movement, and meditation, and it felt familiar to me, though not from this life. I was entranced with the class. Morton was dynamic. At the end of a six to eight hour day we did "spiritual" remote viewing exercises.

Now, when studying with Morehouse, we followed the military protocol he learned while working as a psychic spy for the CIA. (Yes, every government does this, just like cops go to psychics and mediums when they need help on cold cases. I have a friend who worked with the FBI for seven years and helped bring down an FBI top ten terrorist and provided accurate evidence that helped bring in the BTK serial killer. She has laser beam accuracy.) Morehouse insisted that we begin viewing sessions by writing the date and military time down and proceed exactly as he had been trained to do—a very complex system involving controlled stages of collecting psychic data. The process was arduous, fascinating, frustrating, but ultimately satisfying. Some of our sessions took several hours and used up to twenty or more pieces of paper. I felt like I was taking the SAT test all over again.

Morton gave us each a single sheet of paper and condensed the process to fifteen minutes. We "viewed" two targets. I did really well on both and was exhilarated to know that I could get results in a lighter, easier fashion. That being said, I'm grateful to have learned the harder way, too.

After Morton's event, he invited me to join him and other students and friends out for a bite. I was honored, still high on the teachings of the class. Morton lived in California. While in New York that week he invited me to several New Age-y events, and I was grateful to go. Some were better than others. (Actually, they were all kinda crappy and low rent.) Eventually, it became clear that while Morton was married, he was not monogamous, and he made stupid, awkward moves on me that I rebuffed.

One of the weirdo events took place in a Hungarian church basement in Manhattan. I don't remember what Morton discussed (prophecies? alien visitations?) just the odd assortment of mostly Hungarian characters, including one that a new comedian friend there called "Hungarian Shrek." There were two witchy women clad in black. One was emaciated and wore stark, round, black, Philip Johnson type eyeglasses. The other looked like Roseanne Barr from the 1980s. They were both petite, though one was round at the middle with spindly little legs. Both were severe in look and demeanor, and I was wary but intrigued. I prefer my spiritual folk sunny side up.

Turns out skinny gal was author and acclaimed photographer Nancy Burson, who had taught photography at Harvard and developed photographic technology that was eventually appropriated by the FBI to develop the projected aging process which helps identify missing children. So, she's no slouch intellectually or artistically. Still, an odd bird. The other gal was Starr Fuentes, a Mexican Polish witch who wore a large, diamond encrusted star pendant, offset by her perma black garb. I circled both women cautiously, trying to figure out who and what they were.

Years later Nancy held the event at beautiful, safe, calming East West Yoga studio. It was $20. Sold. She was talking about extra terrestrials ("extra celestials" she calls them, or "ECs"). Seems she'd been communicating with and photographing them for a while. I bought her book *Lineage*. It was interesting, and it was there that I first learned of her teacher, the Irish Guru I wrote about in "Rock, Paper, Scissors."

That evening she would also talk about orbs (spirit energy which is sometimes digitally captured by camera, and sometimes seen by people with their eyes, like me, which I detailed in "The Woman with Bubbles on Her Knee"). In *Lineage*, Burson describes a glow in the dark plastic Jesus, a tiny, piece of crap chotchka someone gave her, and how he dances in the dark. He is not battery operated. He is not designed to dance.

I saw a few people I knew at the event (a semi-small world, the New Age community in New York City). It had a homey feel. I sat next to a very friendly young man and liked him immediately. Vinny. A Wall Street guy from Jersey, married with kids. And a medium. Made my day. I loved the incongruity of him. Vinny brought his digital camera. He was ready to capture orbs, or "extra celestials," or whatever showed up in the room that night. Nancy blackened the room to pitch (as a photographer, she had skills in this department). Prior to the darkening she had placed plastic Jesus and Mary (they were about two inches tall each) under a strong Luxo lamp (that's how I remember it, Pixar-loving moi). Her talk was not impressive, nor was her style, being shy, retiring (and weird). Still dressed in all black. Still emaciated. Still wearing those stark, black, Philip Johnson-style eyeglasses. Oh, and the Prema Agni, the motif of her "spiritual teacher," the Irish Guru, around her neck.

    The evening was much ado about nothing. Oh, I forgot! She gave out holy water at the end! I brought a little bottle with me to retrieve mine. It's too embarrassing to talk about now, but basically, she claimed to have "manifested" some gold stuff (don't ask) and said it purified water and raised its vibration sufficiently that it had healing qualities. Listen, in theory, this is all possible in my book. I believe Jesus could do all those fancy tricks they said he did. And Jesus was not alone in being The Christ. The Buddha, any ascended Master, Avatar (who are the Girls, I still want to know?) can do it. The question was, would Nancy's water do it? I had a bum knee. I brought my bottle just in case.

Glo in the Dark Jesus and Mary had soaked up the warm rays of the Luxo long enough. The room went black. It was show time. Drapes were put up over the blinds since New York, even at night, has reams of light pouring in from all directions. Just try seeing a star at night here. We're lucky we see the moon. Or the sun, for that matter.

Vinny was seated to my right, and I recall a sense of anticipation and…boredom. Nancy put Jesus out first. She said that "he *insisted* he go first." Excuse me? Macho much? Not the Jesus I know and love! This was Narcissist Glow in the Dark Jesus. He stood there, all two inches of him. What bodega was he from? He glowed alright, as all glow in the dark thingamajiggies do. I paid $20 for this? This show was incredibly pedestrian, puerile, and dull. But then, I swear…Jesus started to dance! The *merengue*. That's what it looked like to me, and I was in the front row of a not too large room. I turned to Vinny and whispered. "You see him moving?"

"Yup."

Okay. Weird. Stupid. Probably our eyes playing tricks on us, right? Of course! Ridiculous bullshit this. Everything I was seeing was fuzzy. But I was seeing it.

Then she put out Mary (Nancy, of course, being the ultimate puppeteer since she is perpetually clad in disappear-in-the-dark black). Mary appeared out of nowhere and stood next to Our Lord and Saviour, Glow-in–the-Dark Plastic Jesus. I stared at The Blessed Mother. Okay. She started to move, too, but not the same as Jesus, *no*, she was swaying her hips left to right, so, more of a salsa thing going on. (Forgive me if I'm getting the salsa/merengue moves confused.) Bottom line, Jesus was moving forward to back, and Mary was shaking her thang from left to right, a little hip action. Ludicrous, I know. I muttered to Vinny. "Do you see her moving, too?"

"Yes."

"But she's moving differently, right?"

"Right."

Later, Nancy distributed her "holy water." She brought her own diminuitive vessels already apportioned with the liquid; I didn't need mine. She offered *tiny* quantities. I'm not good at estimating—a quarter ounce? She told us once we added it to other water, its healing abilities *kept growing*. Take some of that water and add it to more water. The supply would last forever. I was curious but skeptical of this strange, plastic evening.

Before we came up to receive our samples she announced, "I am not allowed (by whom, she never said) to charge you for this. But I *can* accept donations."

What a relief! Thank goodness "they" allow you to accept donations! My *irritation* was dancing wildly now. I took one sample, no two, and left nothing in her donation envelope. I'd already paid $20 for the evening. That's all she gets for making me stare at plastic.

Still, even with the "whatever" factor of the evening, I wanted to believe the water was special. I added it to a bottle of Smart Water (how smart was I?). I took a sip. Would I grow tall like Alice? Would I shrink like Alice? Nothing happened. I took another sip another day. More light anticipation on my part. Same nothing response. What *was* supposed to happen? Perhaps I might glow in the dark and merengue? Vinny never did get any interesting images from his camera. (Forgive me, Vinny, if I remember this wrong.) Or maybe he emailed me his "interesting" images and I didn't find them so interesting. Finally, in frustration, I downed the entire liter of Holy Smart Water just to get rid of it and the embarrassing memories. Coulda healed me. Coulda killed me. Nothing happened. (You're shocked, I know.)

I LOVE this stuff. This is the Human Mystery. What's real? What's bullshit? It's up to us to figure that out for ourselves. Do I think Burson's a little loopy? Yes. She started selling rag dollies on the web, primitive looking Extra Celestial girls named "Celeste" for $150. Hard to take someone like that seriously. Seriously. Does that negate her photographic brilliance or her visions? No. Would I study with her again? No. I paid for her class, I bought her book, and I drank her damn holy water. What did I get from it? A great fucking story!

Then I took a class with her pal Starr Fuentes. One night. $38. I decided to do so when I learned from her website that she had studied with a curandera in Mexico named Esperanza. I had read about Esperanza in Florinda Donner's amazing books *Shabono* and *Being in Dreaming*. (Florinda was friends with Carlos Castaneda.) I got both books for free when I worked for HarperCollins publishers. Lucky for me, division HarperSanFrancisco published mystical stuff, which I received for free in lieu of an actual paycheck. (Publishing paid notoriously poorly, and given the current digital and audio book markets, I imagine even worse now.) They gave me "monopoly money" to pay my bills.

Starr's class was in a dumpy, fluorescently-lit room probably in the West 20s or 30s. (Strangely, there are lots of spiritual classes in that ugly industrial area, maybe just cause it's cheap, but there are other cheap parts of town.) We were not allowed to ask personal questions that evening. We had to phrase them "generically." She looked around the room. "Who's thinking of multiple orgasms?" Huh? No one answered. (Who would claim that one?) She glowered at us. "Oh, *right*. That would be me." The gal was a comedienne. I appreciated it.

I wanted to know about the crappy married guy, Sean David Morton, the New Age "guru" who seemed to know so much and touched me deeply as a student, but skeeved me out personally.

I piped up, "How can you reconcile someone who seems to know a lot metaphysically but doesn't appear to be a person of integrity?"

She cocked her head to one side like a bird. "Who's thinking of chocolate?" she barked, then looked around the room suspiciously. No one answered. "Oh, right. That's me again." She focused her intense gaze on me. "Did you learn anything?"

"Yes. Yes I did." That was it. I got the gift. Thus endeth the lesson.

CHAPTER 16

THE GYPSY CURSE...
A CAUTIONARY TALE

December 26, 2011

A friend of mine was in town from England. Martin was a lovely, chipper chap who fancied snorkeling and underwater photography and had recently fallen in love with a French girl, Cerise. They met in Europe at a personal growth class. I met him at a similar class in the States, a place I used to adore until I worked there. Despite my disillusionment with their behind the scenes operations, nothing takes away from how much I learned there over the decades as a student. I used their teachings to transform me. However, given my hard-earned, eye-popping insider information, I'll not return. Are you seeing a recurring theme in my writing? Separate the message from the messenger, the wheat from the chaff. *Actually*, regarding real wheat and chaff you *should* keep them together to get roughage and nutrition from the bran and germ. I'm into whole foods, what can I say?

Martin and I studied with a brilliant teacher. The person who taught my teacher was Bruce Di Marsico, deceased, and I urge you to look at his essays on The Option Method Network website. Bruce presents crystal clear guidance on how to examine your beliefs so that they support your happiness instead of hindering it. He taught the *hows* of unconditional love. When we compassionately accept the things we want to change, it is easier to transform them. When we judge things and feel bad about them (the end result of judging), we root ourselves more firmly to the very things we wish to eliminate.

Change can be easy. Growth can be fun. This is not a belief a lot of people hold. They make change harder as a result. Remember, change is inevitable. Growth is optional. And if you're not moving forward, you *are* moving backward. Life is in constant flux. So instead of fighting things, accept them as they are so that you can shift, flow, and move happily towards your wants instead of unhappily away from what you no longer want. There's a huge difference between the two approaches.

Typically, we feel we have to hate things in order to dispense with them, such as political opponents, jobs, excess weight, difficult people. Bruce said, "If you're eating blueberry pie and you decide to switch to cherry, do you have to spit in the blueberry pie first? Can't you just just switch to cherry?"

We spit, damn, curse, flap, flail, and harrumph when we could simply *move on*.

I adore Bruce's teachings and I adore discussing them with friends who are similarly enamored of their beauty, simplicity, and power. Cerise was not in New York with my friend Martin, but a friend of hers, Maria, a Moroccan "seer" was visiting from Paris. Martin was meeting her for tea downtown, and he was hoping she would read for him. I secretly hoped I could meet her too, but he wanted to be alone with her. He told me to meet him downtown when they were done and I did. Maria was still there. She had olive skin and a French Moroccan accent. She was a bit scary to me, almost a bit woozy, with a mysterious demeanor.

"Can I speak to you?" she asked.

I knew what she meant. "Yes," I said, excited that I would get a reading, too.

"You haf problem with men," she said in her thick accent.

Great. Thud. So glad I could be here.

"You haf too many szings, you haf no room for man."

Uh, yes, my home is "thing" heavy. Nice things but many of them. This means I can't date?

"Also, there is old man living inside you."

"Where?" I looked down. What was she talking about? My grandfathers? One died before I was born, the other in the 1980s, and while I loved him, we didn't have a complicated relationship. He wasn't a complicated man. A nice, mystic German, Leo was a ladies' tailor who trained in Paris and fought in World War I. Whenever I visited my German grandparents, Papu gave me paper and pencil to draw with, his newspaper and magazine cartoon collection (they were cut out and taped in a black and white composition notebook) to peruse, and a bag of Hershey's kisses or cashews to take home. My mother told him to back off the nuts and chocolate when I hit puberty. (My skin was fine. It was my weight she was concerned about.) Papu had a long nose, long ears (an indicator of long life), and smoked cigars and pipes, whose scent I love to this day. He had an errant hearing aid he adjusted constantly (and embarrassingly) in the auditorium of our Sunday school, The United Lodge of Theosophists in New York City. Papu's wires and batteries emitted loud, high-pitched squeals that he couldn't hear. But *we* could. Loud and clear.

Anyway, what the heck would Papu be doing "living inside me"? Made no sense. Maria's demeanor was ominous and dark. The three of us left the tea room and walked around the East Village. Martin was taking me to dinner in gratitude for my putting him up, and Maria decided he could take her, too. I was not pleased. I was disturbed by her reading *and* her pushiness. We went to my favorite Italian restaurant.

She sat next to me and observed the clientele. "Thees ees a lesbian restaurant."

What was she talking about? This was a Mario Battali joint with couples and families. Did gays and lesbians go there? Undoubtedly, but it was no lesbian hot spot. She brushed my thigh with her hand under the table. Aaah, yes. I could see her point. It was a lesbian restaurant *now*. I edged away from her on the banquette.

We ordered glasses of wine and as she reached for hers she tipped it over to the left. This was a nice joint, complete with pristine white linen and superb service. Her sloppy behavior was galling, but she managed to catch the glass with her left hand. The glass then tipped to the right. Hollywood special effects could not easily recreate this. She caught it again with her right hand and this time managed to hurl the glass in a 360 spin the likes of which I have never seen before or since. The wine was now airborne, and like paint from a spin-art machine, her red wine sprayed in a complete circle, dousing me, Martin, and the white tablecloth. Our lesbian waitress was not amused.

Maria laughed. "The spirits must be thirsty! Ha ha ha ha ha!"

Bruja. I was annoyed. So much for my classy, pleasant dinner with chipper Martin. No, I was saddled with murky Maria. She invited another compadre, François, to join us at the lesbian restaurant. French and gay, François was familiar with the puppeteer that Martin and I were going to see after dinner. François worked in the art world, gave me his card, and asked me to stay in touch. I wasn't sure why.

I was in a dark mood as the two of us headed over to the theatre.

"Are you alright?" Martin inquired with his darling English accent and genuinely caring demeanor.

"No. I'm not." Who wants to be told they can't date because they have too many objets d'art? "I don't understand about the old man."

He stopped cold on West Broadway and stared at me. "You don't?"

I shook my head, forlorn.

He was incredulous. "You *don't?*" He reminded me of the old icon I had just dated (as described in "A Tale of Two Soldiers"). Martin had met him. He had comforted me when I cried about the relationship.

"Oh! Oh, God. I didn't think of that. You're right. I think *old man* I think *grandpa*, not boyfriend. Ha. Right. Old man. Yes, he is. Old. Living *inside* me? Uck!" I was determined to do a ceremony to "cut the cord" that night, after the theatre.

We saw a show by Basil Twist (an innovative puppeteer) and Joey Arias, a character I knew of from the 1970s when Fiorucci graced my neighborhood. Joey was friends with singer Klaus Nomi (you saw Klaus' strangely powdered visage in Jagermeister ads) and I saw them both since I worked in a tiny clothing shop named Suzuya across the street from Fiorucci, where Joey and Klaus hung out. I sold Whittall and Javits hats at Suzuya the summer after graduating high school.

When Martin and I got home, I ripped my house apart. Martin's not a giant, but he's taller than me. "Could you grab that, oh, and those?" I asked as I tore things off walls and shelves and threw them into bags. It was perfectly clear what needed to go. Stuff that no longer served me. Goofy funny stuff to represent my sillier side. Too many crafts, pitchers, and vases. Lovely, yes. Excess. Yes. I ended up collecting forty-five shopping bags to donate to the Salvation Army. Not all that night, but I laid the groundwork for the demolition that evening. No ashtray was gonna get in the way of my love life, dammit.

Around the same time (roughly) I attended my first séance. A male medium approached and asked if he could "come to me." (This is proper séance protocol to make sure you're willing to receive a message.) This fellow was a dead ringer for William Quan Judge, the co-founder with Madame Blavatsky of the Theosophical movement, which comprised the spiritual upbringing of my childhood.

"WQJ" saw the "old man" in my aura. He described the warped personality perfectly, but perceived him physically as he was in the 1970s, when he achieved notoriety, not the old man he is today. Time and space are totally relative (or irrelevant) in the ethers.

"Is he dead?" I inquired, hopefully. He couldn't tell. "Is there a message?" I asked. He shook his head. Then why was he here, I wondered? Don't you have to be dead to show up at a seance?

"WQJ" said that this was a very angry person, a rebel, and that he looked like an East Village hippie.

I said, "It wasn't the East Village, but you're close. You got him." At least he was outside, not inside me this time.

James Van Praagh, the (deservedly) well-known medium I've studied with three times said, "When someone is in your aura they are thinking about you." So I had confirmation from two strangers that, A) he was thinking about me and, B) *living inside me.* Crikey.

I used Martin as my witness. I addressed the ceremony to him. "Out, out damn spot! You were near *impossible* to pin down when I was seeing you, but now that it's over, you're haunting me? How dare you! And you're not even dead!" He always had a lot of nerve.

I took a piece of rope to symbolize our connection and a sharp knife to sever it. I was on fire. I spoke words forever cutting this old geezer from my life. How dare he live in me, whatever that meant! Could I charge him back rent?

Several weeks later I got a message from François, the gay French friend of the Moroccan gypsy Maria. He said Maria had sent something from Paris for me. My stomach tightened. Why would she send me anything? What witchcraft was this, and why? What did she want from me? I asked him if he knew what it was.

"Something to help your love life."

I left the house immediately. My housecleaning efforts had produced no discernable results.

I trekked all the way over to Chelsea where the art gallery he worked in was. This was about as far west you could go in Manhattan without dropping off into the Hudson River. My fears were assuaged immediately when I met the charming half-European half-Asian boss of the Frenchman. She was warm, funny, and endearing. An Earth Mother. They offered me tea. I felt right at home with both of them.

The mysterious Moroccan had sent me a single red fishnet glove. Why one? What was I to do with it? He told me to put it in my bedroom. I was grateful. Feeling empowered, warm and fuzzy after spending time with the nurturing Earth Mother who made up for the mysterious Moroccan, I trudged back home. I dutifully put the red glove in a drawer in my bedroom.

Well, nothing changed in my love life. I began to wonder whether the "gift" was a charm or a curse. I hadn't asked her for anything. Then again, my friend hadn't asked her to dinner that night, either. She had her own, strange ways.

I met with an adorable college pal from New Hampshire, of Italian and Lebanese descent. He's exceedingly funny, bright, and good-looking. I told him about the mysterious glove and my concern about it.

He responded, "*I* have a gypsy curse."

I was shocked. "What?"

He pointed to his pot belly and said, "*This* is a gypsy curse."

I burst out laughing. "How is *that* a gypsy curse?"

He'd always been gorgeous and slender, but as the years progressed, he'd developed a gut. He'd also become a chef. He explained how when he was in high school his mother, an ob-gyn, once had a gypsy patient who offered to "read" for the doctor and gave predictions for all three of her kids. About my friend she said only "when he is older he will have a weight problem." My pal was infuriated that his mother was satisfied with that answer. That's his fortune? With all his genius as a writer, editor, humorist, and chef, the only item of note from his future was a pot belly? We eyed his "gypsy curse" together.

I never saw the mysterious Moroccan again. Martin married Cerise. The couple remain friends with Maria. I developed a friendship with the French art guy due to our mutual interest in the occult (Don't get scared, children, occult simply means "that which is hidden." It implies no evil of any kind). Over time, strange developments occurred in our relationship which I have outlined in Chapter 19.

I became convinced that Maria's energy was not good, and that just because she had "vision" did not mean that she was "of the light." I've known far too many psychics that have ability but no scruples, powers but no manners, gifts but no humility, and heart but no compassion. Spirituality trumps psychic ability any day. As we grow spiritually, as our heart centers expand, so naturally do our psychic abilities, just as a toddler organically learns to walk. Vision is our birthright, our heritage. I will always value my own thoughts over anyone else's. Never let someone else's opinion of you, or prediction for you (unless it is peachy keen) become your reality. Honor yourself. Trust yourself.

I threw out the glove. I didn't burn it because I didn't want whatever spell she put on it to seep into the ethers. It went to a dump in Staten Island.

My cousin Genia said, "Something was wrong with it. Everyone knows that charms to attract love come in *twos*, not *ones*." (For obvious reasons if you want to be part of a couple.)

Years later I had dinner with my college friend. I had seen him in the interim, but this time I was shocked. He was thin again! I said, "What happened to your gypsy curse?"

He said, "Oh. I'm eating less."

That was that. The power of suggestion (and his overindulging in food and drink) had allowed him to grow a gut. He's not the first man, or chef, to develop one. But his strength as a human allowed him to kill it, too. He ate half his entrée and took scant sips of our truly crappy happy hour "wine."

Never give your power away to anyone else. And if you do, remember you can take it right back.

CHAPTER 17

SATHYA SIGH...BABA AU RHUM

December 31, 2011

I never met him. I never would have. I don't like crowds or hording masses of worshipping people. I first heard of him when I saw his photo in Nancy Burson's book *Lineage*. He was presented as her guru's guru. I found both men's smiling photos to be intoxicating. They seemed to be oozing love. Or something.

As I delved into the world of Burson's guru, an Irish bloke, I got exposed to, if not the world, then at least the visage of the guru's guru, Sathya Sai Baba, of India. His photo was often venerated, as was Irish bloke's, even when Irish bloke himself was present, a bit of overkill to be sure. I thought we got this whole idolatry thing straightened out a long time ago, that whole "no false idols" thing. But, no, even the Church is full of them. People worship icons. People worship shoes, for God's sake.

One of Sai Baba's little tricks (I know, I know, his followers called them "miracles") was manifesting dirt out of thin air. Now, if you are a magical manifestor, can't you do better than dirt? I've written about apports before—magical manifestations such as rose petals, gems, and seed pearls. These are precious apports, and I'd be pleased to have them land on my lap. But dirt?

Baba's dirt was something called vibhuti, a whitish/grayish ash, something you'd clean out of your fireplace, or better yet, what I dump out of my HEPA vacuum cleaner canister. This is a miracle? Only if you vacuum my house first, Guru! It's considered "holy ash" and is derived from burned incense (or the Dyson Animal).

So I watched this Netflix DVD last night, *Rod Serling Presents: Sathya Sai Baba, Man of Miracles*. The DVD was produced in 2005, but the footage was from the late '60s or early '70s by the looks of it, (and from the fact that Serling was narrating). Here are the miracles I witnessed: 1) Tiny lacquered photos of the Guru (these would be icons) about the size of a dime sat in the palm of someone's hand. Within seconds they "wept" holy nectar. (I wasn't sure whether to put "wept" or "holy nectar" in quotes. You decide.) Now, having performed on stage and in film I've seen a special effect or two. The thick liquid looked like glycerin to me (what doubles for tears in film). So "something" on the back of the icon melted in the heat of the palm and released within seconds. Some miracle, huh? Besides, what's the significance of a trinket that cries? What's *it* got to be sad about?

People followed a man in an orange muumu with an *enormous* afro because he did parlor tricks? He didn't heal people. He attracted huge crowds—throngs of people, both poor and supremely rich—and amassed a fortune as a result. I suppose that *is* a miracle of sorts.

For his next "act," Baba produced vibhuti on stage. Wasn't a stage the *first* giveaway that this was a performance, not an act of God? His magician's assistant (an old Indian guy, not a cute girlie in fishnets) held a two gallon terracotta pot upside down while Baba stuck his hand up, swirled it around, and *lo*, out poured a cloud of ash! Baba smiled and moved his hand some more, and behold…talcum powder! Dust! Dirt! It's a miracle! The pot was packed with fine ash capable of being loosened by a circulating human hand. You'd think this was The Second Coming. The vibhuti was dumped unceremoniously on some poor statue, heaps and heaps of the powder poured out. All I could think was, "Now, *who's* gonna clean that up?" The man made messes, not miracles.

He also manifested necklaces sporting his lacquered visage out of "thin air," something that was "not easy to do," commented Serling. Haven't magicians been pulling trinkets out of sleeves for decades? This is not new technology. His devotees were not limited to Indians. He had his white (and Irish) followers too, including Isaac Tigrett, founder of the Hard Rock Café, who gave him

$108 million. When Baba died on April 24, 2011, at the age of 84, he left a fortune of 8.9 *billion* dollars, having received foreign donations of $19.5 million in 2009 alone. Nice work for a man in a robe. What can I say? The man had fans. And I believe this Faqir was a Fake.

Here's what struck me as hideous, terrible, and obvious: despite his setting up "charitable institutions" (you certainly have to make an *effort* to look legit, don't you?) these mass events were all about HIM and his 'fro. Ego, ego, ego! It was hero worship, pure and simple, except what kind of a hero throws dirt on people and distributes cheap jewelry with his likeness on it like a car salesman handing out pens?

I assisted a casting agent a couple of times and one of the auditionees handed me his publicity kit. He was a trés-tattooed body-builder and he offered me a miniature tool kit with his contact info all over it. Included was a red, white, and blue emery board "tattooed" with his slogan. How was Bhagwan Sri Sathya Sai Baba any different? The guy's a saint and he's palming cheap jewelry. Is this Puttaparthi, or New Orleans?

Did Jesus hand out Jesus paraphernalia? Did he walk around with paintings of himself? And when he did perform a "trick" miracle (that water into wine thing) at *least* it was useful. Wine, or micro particle effluvia, anyone? Jesus didn't put on a show. This Baba guy was a showman, pure and simple. And so is his acolyte, who I wrote about in "Rock, Paper, Scissors." This spiritual rock-star bullshit really pisses me off, and what's baffling is how many go for it. The accusations that "Baba au Rhum" sexually abused boys and young men received attention from the BBC in 2004, but was never investigated in India. We don't like to question our saints or priests about sexual improprieties, do we, whether they're in a muumu or a football jersey.

In contrast, I warily approached another one of these crowd pleasers. Why? Because it was a free event. I didn't have to travel to India. She came to me. Amma is a famous gal. She's known as "the hugging lady." Is she a guru, a saint? All I know is people worship her. I don't worship anyone. I explore. I see what someone has and decide if it is useful to me. Preferably, dark chocolate is involved.

A personal growth friend was visiting me from Holland, and she encouraged me to go "get hugged" by Amma while she was in New York, at yes, the Manhattan Center again, on West 34th Street. (I've mentioned before, lots of woo woo and New Age-y things take place there, as well as at the New Yorker Hotel around the corner on 8th Avenue.) Huge throngs of people waited in line to see her, as if for a rock concert, and "homey don't play that." I don't wait in line for hours for anything. Not my style.

I had an audition in the city and then a commercial shoot in New Jersey that afternoon. It was July. I wore white linen pants and blouse, and platform Kork-Ease sandals, which I've sported since the '70s (even trudging through the woods in them at camp in Michigan). It was a beautiful day. Now, I believe in miracles and prayer, and I experience and use them in my life. It turned out that the Manhattan Center was conveniently located to my New

Jersey pickup, and time-wise, I had forty-five minutes to fight the hordes, get a hug, and run to the van. Not the way the teeming masses generally got to see her. The lines of devotees went around the block.

It was a crapshoot at best, but feeling adventurous and not at all needy, I decided to give it a go. By late morning when I arrived there were no crowds waiting outside. A promising sign. But the throngs were waiting *inside*, and they had all taken a number. I was asked at the door if it was my first time. "Yes." That meant I was given some priority since there were a lot of repeat customers inside, just clamoring for a second or third hug since their last pilgrimage. I presented my case. "I know this may sound crazy, but I only have forty-five minutes. What are the odds that I could get a hug?" Instead of laughing at me, that person ushered me to another person who ushered me to another person. I repeated my question amidst the thousands of people sitting there. As it so happened, I looked like a devotee in my summer whites from CP Shades and Old Navy.

A lady took me to the front of the room, and within thirty minutes I was on my knees and instructed to wipe off my makeup so it didn't get all over Amma when she hugged me. (She pressed people's faces to her ample bosom which was clothed in white.) I was like "hell to the no, I'm going to a shoot!" (Being an extra, not a principal in the commercial, I had to put my own makeup on beforehand.) There's God, and there's work. I blotted my lipstick. That's as far as I'd go.

I'm not an "on my knees" kinda gal unless I'm looking for something on the floor, but since knees were the vogue (unless you had a physical problem impeding your kneeling), I went along with their little game. There were all types of people here. A lot of Indians and white folk dressed like Indians (you know, the tie dye thing, turbans, bindis, bracelets, assumed Indian names). I took it like the circus it was. There were vendors selling Amma souvenirs, saris, and shawls as well as vegetarian food. Amma runs charities, too, and this is one of the ways she funds them.

As I knelt my way up to her, I got a closer look at the goings on. Her entourage pushed us efficiently through the feed mill.

"Here's a tissue, take your make up off!"

"Move up!"

"Get ready!"

"You're next!"

It was a finely tuned machine. An Indian couple with two small children was directly ahead of me and an older white woman was ahead of them. I watched Amma look with pure and deep love at the white haired lady and gently touch her face. I got choked up. Amma pulled the lady's face tenderly to her heart and held her there in a long embrace. This tiny plump lady in her fifties has hugged millions of people. That's what she does. That's her job.

"GO!"

Her handlers, one on either side of me, pushed me firmly forward like I was about to bungee jump. Her white garb was already covered in makeup and schmutz from people's faces. She took my head, turned it to the left and mashed it forcefully into her chest. She had a vice grip. I could sorta see out of one eye but my nostrils were embedded in her vestments. She was smothering me. The room was filled with noise, and she semi-yelled in her language to a clump of assistants at her left. (There was also a video person taping all this.) From the tone of her voice, I could have sworn she was ordering a large pepperoni pizza and a Diet Coke. She babbled loudly what sounded to be chitchat. Oh, this was sacred, all right. Then she took my head and turned it abruptly to the other side, as if flipping a pancake, and proceeded to shove my nose back into her bosom. I was now suffocating to the right. It was surreal. Like a big politician grabbing your hand and near breaking it as he shakes it and says, "Hi! Howareya! Hope I can count on you in the election!" This was factory farm hugging.

She lifted my head slightly with both hands and whispered into my right ear. I recall a lot of MMMM's, so, a Hindi version of "hummana hummana, hummana, hummana." And with that, I was jettisoned off. To the right, where this California lady, a veteran huggee wearing tie dye who had helped me get to the front of the hordes, now warned me, "Be careful. You might want to keep your high heels off. The energies are *very* strong. You might feel light headed."

Yeah, right. I thanked her (and others) for helping me that day. I took a few steps and my head started spinning. What the hell? I was woozy. Light headed. Dizzy. Power of suggestion? I was certainly no dreamy-eyed convert. I was more of a silent heckler. The sensation lasted for thirty minutes. In the interim, I had to shove my platform sandals on and hit the pavement to catch my connection to Jersey.

I had no conclusions to form about the Amma thing. It was like being in a crowded train station with brief smushing, suffocation, and some muttering. Other than the miracle of getting in and out so quickly and the thirty minutes of disorientation après, there was nothing so special about it.

On set in New Jersey, I watched pretty girls slurp Campbell's soup seductively, placidly, as if the liquid lifted them to Nirvana itself. With the money they were making, I don't doubt that it did. Now *that* was sacred nectar. When it was all over, I waited to go home on the train platform. It was a beautiful, quiet, bright summer evening, and I was surrounded by trees and sky. You don't see the sky so much in Manhattan.

Months later, I was at a healing session with another character. He was highly focused in another realm as he hovered over my (clothed) body.

He paused. "Are you a devotee of Amma?" he inquired.

"No," I said, startled by the question. "Why?"

"I feel her energy swirling around inside you," he responded.

"You do?" I was shocked that he picked this up. "Well—" I paused. "I *was* hugged."

His observation was confirmation to me that there *was* something to the Amma phenomenon. If a stranger who knew nothing about me could sense this energy within…well, something was verifiable, wasn't it? That's when this stuff starts coming together—when you get outside confirmations, and repeatedly, as is often the case.

So this Amma lady, she's got followers. Lots of 'em. She sells trinkets. She has charities. I don't know who or what she is, really. Is she a healer? Maybe. A saint? Could be. One of her handlers said she neither slept nor ate. Really? Then how come she's so fat, another miracle? Is she an avatar? That's between her and God. Do I need to be hugged again? Nah, I'm good. Besides…her energy is still swirling around inside me.

I don't sense that she is a charlatan. There is much to recommend her, having watched *her* documentary (although I only gave it two out of five stars on Netflix). Be forewarned, ladies and gentlemen, I've read several predictions from trusted spiritual sources that in the midst of all the crises going on as this world shifts out of the crap we've been swimming in to a world of effortless ease, beauty, and grace (you heard me right) that some charismatic charmer (I suspect a male) will appear out of nowhere and seem to have the answers to all the world's problems. Don't you believe it. Be discerning, my friends. Eyes and ears open. Elvis has left the building.

CHAPTER 18

PETER, PAUL, AND ME-ARY (I MEAN ME)

January 2, 2012

I know several channelers, including two Peters and a Paul (only ten more apostles to go!). One Peter is very abstemious, slight of build, and when I went to his home for a private reading ten years ago, extraordinarily "zen" (read spare, or he couldn't afford any furniture). He looked like he did yoga all day (or couldn't afford food). He wrote a simple guidebook about physical and spiritual health, including the evils of white flour and sugar. (I concur, they are the *real* "White Devil" now that the KKK is out of the running.) These empty calories are addictive drugs that suppress our feelings when we stuff them down.

I used to attend Peter's group channelings when their location was convenient.

Paul is a very human fellow. He diets and complains about being single. He has a dog. He teaches college. He's also an extraordinary channel. I attended his group channelings from time to time for the better part of a year.

The other Peter is a horse of a different color. Young, vibrant, in great shape, he goes to the gym regularly and works like a dog. He's always running around. I met him at a séance. It was a pretty crappy séance, truth be told, or "message circle" as they're also sometimes called. I'd been to circles where the messages were of a higher nature than, "Your dead uncle likes your jacket." The energy is only as good as the folks in the room. This one felt like a waste of time, giving meaning to the disclaimer, "for entertainment purposes only." Except that it was boring, so even that conceit was a wash. However, Peter had been offering messages that impressed me. They seemed insightful and heartfelt.

The evening was coming to a close. I raised my hand when the "Reverend" running the group (reverends are a dime a dozen in these spiritualist groups), asked who had not yet received a message. It was very dark in the room, but I could see/sense where the voices were coming from. Peter, seated somewhere to my right, perked up to speak when I raised my hand.

But another medium piped up first.

"Yes, Reverend Carmelita?" said "Reverend Whatever-Whatever" running the show.

Ms. Rev C. was pushing 60 but she dressed like Charro in her twenties. She was ready for clubbing with a dress cut low (both front and back), long orangey-blonde hair (or a wig), heels (of course), and a lotta makeup. That's fine if it's Saturday night in the Bronx. If you're going to assume the moniker "reverend" at a spirit circle, couldn't you try to dress a little *reverentially?* You don't have to wear a turtleneck, but, honestly, do you have to wear a push-up bra?

She intoned like Charro, too, as she gave me my message. "Ju grandfathah is heah an' he say dat ju are *emotional disturb."*

Thanks, Charro! Not *exactly* what Papu would have said, but in fact, I could work with the full message that she gave me without holding it against her.

You have to be savvy about psychic messages. No one picks up or presents the full enchilada. Anyone worth their psychic salt can get a piece of the puzzle, sometimes several pieces. I do not discount a reading just because some of it is off. (If *all* of it is off, that's another matter.) You don't dismiss a meteorologist if something in her report is not exact, because there are many constantly-shifting variables that contribute to weather patterns.

There are many psychic variables, too. The future is not written in stone. A sensitive picks up possibilities and probabilities, not "the future." There is no such thing as "the future." As *you* change day by day (And don't kid yourself. You are not who you were even *yesterday* unless you are a total slug.) your alternate futures shift accordingly, sometimes minute by minute depending on what's going on in your life. If you're on a downward trajectory with dark thoughts, feelings, and behaviors, you're plotting a dark course. As soon as you straighten up and fly right, your future possibilities lighten and brighten.

So, back to interpreting psychic/mediumistic readings. First of all, do you know the difference between them yet? All mediums are psychic (i.e. "sensitive" to Spirit), but not all psychics are mediums (people who communicate with individual spirits). The reader (your psychic or medium) brings her own filters, thoughts, and personality to the message she's giving. Two mediums can present very different versions of the same message from the same spirit. It's like the game of telephone. The initial sentence usually has nothing to do with the final message that gets relayed, hence the humor. (But not so funny if you really want to know where that last will and testament was stashed.)

Don't forget to bring that same sense of humor to your readings. People take this stuff *way* too seriously (including me, at times). We look to the psychic or medium as the Voice of God. They're not. They're one-part how strong their connection is to Spirit generally (think wireless signal), one-part how clear and focused they are this particular hour, and one-part what they had for lunch. Burp. Yes, it's all part of the mix. It's a weather report, not the Gospel. You're the authority in your life. *Never forget that.* No one knows you better than yourself, no matter what patterns or possibilities someone picks up on.

A medium is an interpreter. Remember that translations are subject to *interpretation*, just as different versions of the Bible are, including what Jesus said. Some people think he said, "Love and don't kill," while others think he said, "Kill the ones you don't love, then blame it on me!"

With any message, teaching, or piece of advice, take what works for you and discard what doesn't. And *don't* go to storefront "psychics" who have windows filled with neon lights, chakra posters, crystals, and shit. They're scam artists. They'll put a curse on you just to charge you to take it off.

So, back to Reverend "Cuchi Cuchi's" message. I am not "emotionally disturbed" (as she indicated) but I *am* very emotional. She mentioned my negativity and judgmentalness. I can own that and I've been working on those qualities. So, I put her words into my handy cryptography translator and created this message for myself: "Take a chill pill. Be more loving and compassionate." But I still wanted to know what that young man was going to say.

When the lights went up I approached him. "Excuse me. Did you have a message for me?"

"Yes," he said.

I had to wait since it seemed he had messages for lots of people, lots of socializing to do, or both. Regardless, when I got my message, it was worth the wait. It was insightful, relevant, reassuring, and he was a total stranger to me. James Van Praagh calls this "survival evidence mediumship," the ability to provide information that is so specific only the person in spirit and the person receiving the message could know it. Peter gave me his business card. He was a VP for Chase Bank.

I saw him maybe three to five times in similar situations, including my psychic development group where he channeled for free. He went into deep trance during which his conscious mind was down for the count. When he came to he remembered nothing. Several powerful energies spoke through him, each with a discernable change of pacing, energy, voice, and topic. They gave specific messages to individuals and inspiring lectures to the group. But mostly it was Peter's guide Hieronymous who came through and did the communicating in an odd voice that struck me as a cross between Yoda and the Minister in *The Princess Bride* with a speech impediment. Hieronymous knew all about me, where Peter did not (I did not socialize with him). Hieronymous's insights were invaluable, including a warning that a natural disaster would hit New York within thirty days (this was a few weeks before Hurricane Irene) and his prodding me, "How's that book going?" before I had written a book, or even started blogging. Score.

A Latino kid from the Bronx, Peter had become a VP at Chase by his late twenties. He presented an interesting mix. His English wasn't great (on the order of "I axed him a question") but he seemed sincere, bright eyed, and bushy-tailed. While he was attractive, he wasn't quite my type and was too young. So I introduced him to a very sweet young friend, also a medium. He took to her, but she was skeptical without giving me specifics.

"Something's off," she said.

I decided she was too sensitive. She picked up negativity a lot of the time. Some of it was dead on, since it was in my life and I could validate it. I couldn't validate the stuff going on in his life. I just liked the guy.

His channeling was magical. Frankly, it had nothing to do with him other than that his body was the vehicle Spirit used to speak through. He didn't drink, he seemed squeaky clean, and I felt like a lush next to him. He was always on the run. He did readings, had a corporate job, and was getting *his* very own "Reverend" certificate from the psychic organization that ran the séances. If you can't guess already, I'm not impressed with the Reverend title. I know too many of 'em who are neither reverent nor inspirational, and some of them are not even pleasant people, though they may be fabulous mediums and psychics. Why can't they just leave it at that?

I'm also perturbed by spiritualist mediums obsessed with their appearance, from fake tans, too much hair gel, tight dresses, plastic surgery, and trendy clothes. There's nothing wrong with looking decent, but if you are devoted to Spirit, shouldn't you be more focused on sanctity and less concerned with "bringing sexy back?" I'm not suggesting nuns' habits, but do you have to look like you're hooking while working a spiritual event? There's far too much ego in these groups and not enough humility. Nothing wrong with being human, but keep that ego (and your fake tan) in check! I believe spiritual development is *far* more important than psychic development. There is no reason the two cannot go hand in hand.

So this young man, it seemed, wanted to be a motivational speaker. I was disappointed to learn that. I loved his channeling and wanted him to do more of that. I felt that channeling was his strong suit, not giving speeches with his "dese, dems, and dose" dialect. He offered a free two-day seminar on "abundance," and I went to support him. While his energy was vibrant and bright, he was preaching to the choir and said nothing new, or frankly, interesting. It seemed he fancied himself the next Tony Robbins. I told him that if he wanted to be a public speaker, he should get a dialect coach and clean up his speech. I "axed" him if he would offer channeling workshops or groups, so that I could benefit from what I considered to be his ace in the pocket and greatest gift. He said he'd let me know.

He claimed that part of his trepidation to channel more was that he didn't know *how* he was being used while he was "out." Were customers using him to get winning lottery numbers? I had two semi-private readings with him that were remarkable, and I sent him the audio so that he could hear what had transpired. There was nothing untoward. In fact, it was all very beautiful, high-level stuff.

On a personal note, he had a vexing habit of not returning emails, even when I was trying to book an appointment with him. Unprofessional. Inexplicable. You work at a bank, you are running your own enterprise, and your new email address has the word "truth" in it? Have some integrity. When he finally offered a channeling group on portal day 11/11/11, I was interested in going but had other plans (see Chapter 8, "Batman and Jose"). I told him to pencil in a spot for me in the event I could rearrange my schedule. When I tried to secure a spot, he was not sure he had one. I had asked him to "please get back to me either way." To my disappointment, he did not. I went ahead with my original plans for the evening.

When he channeled, Archangels came through. You can snort and roll your eyes if you like, but I remain convinced. Varied energies with beautiful messages came through, each with unique voice, quality, and pacing. I was in a semi-private channeled session when another person asked what Jesus's most important message was. I snorted and rolled *my* eyes. I thought, "What a dumb-ass question. *Everything* Jesus said was pithy and powerful." His motif was love, love, love, yourself and others, and he said it a million different ways. What was Jesus's bestselling sound bite, "the phrase that pays," *The Top of the Pops*, his biggest hit? Please.

When the energies within his body were shifting (it was a macabre process to be sure), I didn't know *what* was going on. Was he choking? Was he dying? Could he breathe? It was different with each new energy coming through. This time his body went stiff as a board, as if he were stretched out on a diving board. His head tilted back in the chair as he arched backward. A deep voice boldly emanated from him and spoke: "I AM THE LIGHT OF THE WORLD."

Ta da. That was it? Out of all of Jesus's hit singles, I'm not sure that's the one I would have selected. But since I was slowly absorbing what was going on and since he had embodied Archangels Michael and Ariel before (Ariel sounded as wispy as Michael Jackson), as well as St. Francis of Assisi, it slowly dawned on me, "Was *that* the big JC? Are you kidding me? Did he come in just for the pop quiz?" I sat there stunned. Peter came to and slowly adjusted to consciousness. Vacating your body is not the easiest thing, although he claimed it always gave him energy instead of depleting him.

He sat there quietly with his head in his hands. I saw him wipe his eyes, then heard him sniffle. Not wanting to interfere, I waited then gently asked, "Are you all right?"

His head still down he replied, "Yeah."

It was obvious now he was crying. I offered him a tissue.

He used it. "I just feel so much love. I've never felt so much love." And he sat there, tears streaming down his face.

I touched his shoulder. "Do you know what happened?" I asked. "Do you know who was here?"

He shook his head.

"I think it was the big J.C. Hieronymous was asked what Jesus's most important teaching was, and it seems as if maybe the big guy answered the question himself. 'I Am The Light Of The World,' he said." I guess it's not a bad sentiment if you had to pick one. It was growing on me.

Peter started sobbing as the enormity of it hit him. He said, "Thank you, thank you, thank you, thank you, you guys."

He was thanking us for the session. What did we do? We attracted the energies that came in. Apparently his other sessions were not all of this caliber.

Time went by, and I sent the guy two emails. A simple response would have been nice, but I received nothing, as usual. Then, the floodgates opened. I got 26 emails from him. I was confused, then shocked, then disturbed. The first seemed to be a response from him to a person from an online dating site. Nothing about this email was to me, except I seemed to be bcc'd on it. I let him know immediately via email, "Somehow I got bcc'd on this, thought you should know." Next, I got an email with a list of nearly 100 girls' names. They were defined by type, age, and race. It said, "If your name is not on this list it's because you joined after (a certain date)."

My name was not on the list. I wrote him again, immediately. "I do not want to be on this list!"

Then a torrent of emails was unleashed. They were filthy, dirty, pornographic, and disgusting. There was a nude photo of Peter, starring his privates standing at attention. Oh, Lord. Emails describing "it," what he did with it, what he thought girls wanted him to do with it. Seemed he emailed a different girl every minute. I was appalled.

I'm not a prude. In fact, I believe sex is sacred. Not like you have to be married to have it (Who says married sex is sacred? It is only if your marriage is.) But love and sex combined can create powerful energy. Healing energy. Uplifting energy. Enlightening energy. This does not apply to anonymous, nameless, faceless stuff, the kind he was selling and buying. (Metaphorically, I hope, although who the hell knows). I looked at every email and my morale sank deeper and deeper. I felt dirty. I went to bed disturbed. I woke up disturbed.

Now I know many of you are going to think this guy is an out and out shyster, and I'm an out and out idiot for believing in him. I never believed in *him*. I believed in the messages that came *through* him. There is a big difference. Have you ever heard of a professional genius who was also a private asshole? Of course you have. The world is full of them. We are all complex, multi-faceted beings and the point is not to judge, but to *discern*. I don't have to judge him for what he's doing personally, but nor will I associate with him again. And now I know why the spirits have to knock the kid out cold before they can talk through him. He's got some low level shit going on.

This Reverend who also calls himself a Dr. (which is ridiculous, since he's neither an M.D. nor a PhD) is a bona fide vehicle of spirit. He's also an amoral pervert and sex addict from what I can tell. He sent out two emails the next day (no apology of course). "My account was hacked! Don't open any emails from me!"

Ha! Too late. I'd already seen Peter's peter and it's not an image I'll soon forget. What a stark (naked) contrast to the squeaky clean mama's boy he presented himself to be. And there I was feeling like a lush next to him. I'll take my glass of wine over whatever lurid energy he's wallowing in. Sure, you can be a nice guy and have sex. But not with hundreds of people. Not in my book. Sorry. What I saw was depraved. There I go judging again! Well, that's my prerogative.

He also admitted in one of the "sex" emails to a specific girl, to lying about where he worked, saying that it was some dinky bank in Flushing, Queens, not Chase on Wall Street. So what about that business card he gave me? I guess he had it printed somewhere. So much for "the truth."

Someone told me my lesson was that I needed to become more "sensitive" like my psychic girl friend who picked up something "being off" about him. I'm not real big on people telling me what my lessons are. I rely on myself for that. I stand by my assessment that he is not a fraud. He is a mass of contradictions and a liar. He's no reverend (I don't care if he has a stupid certificate or not) and he's certainly no doctor. However, I do not rue my association with him. In fact, I'm grateful for it. He is a fascinating conundrum. Like Salieri in *Amadeus* I wonder, "Why did God pick this pervert to speak through?" I can't answer that. But my association with him is over.

One of my lessons is to grasp that we are all human. And that we are all divine. How we manifest that balance is up to us, but first we must grasp the awareness that we are more than our ego and our body. In the past, I had a tendency to put people on pedestals only to see them topple. What a great, *great* lesson for me to witness my idols vaporize. It's not that others don't have value, gifts, and brilliance, it's that *they don't have more than me*. No one has what I have. No one knows what I know. No one is more important than I am. That goes for you, too. Honor, respect, and cherish yourself. Build yourself up instead of tearing yourself down. I'm not talking about ego. I'm talking about good, clean, humble, brilliant self-esteem. The kind that thoroughbred race horses have.

So who do you think hacked Peter's account? It could be one of the many women, though from what I could tell, from some of their responses back to him (I was privy to the whole thread), their interests were as lurid as his. So why would they care? It could have been Spirit. He was not living in integrity, and he was using his pulpit as "reverend/dr." to accrue clients as well as conquests (or were they customers? I shudder to think). The final answer is the one I like. He was "Punk'd" by God.

I'm not here to judge him. I'm not here to throw stones. I'm fascinated by the intense swirling of sacred and profane within this one human. God speaks through all of us. Just because the messenger is not in integrity doesn't mean that when he's "working," he's not connected to high energies. Didn't Jesus wash Mary Magdalene's feet? The Lord works in mysterious ways.

Here's a little math for you: Sex + Love = Heaven. Heart + Hand = Heal the World. Think with your heart. Feel with your head. WEAREALLONE. Shalom.

CHAPTER 19

THE CHEESE THIEF (A SCARY STORY)

January 4, 2012

This is my own personal *Blair Witch Project*, or "Blitch Witch Project," as one of my outrageous gym teachers mispronounced it. He couldn't pronounce synopsis either. He tried a few times then settled on "synospis." The reason I was discussing *The Blair Witch Project* and the word synopsis with my kickboxing teacher is because he asked me to work on a horror film with him, which I did, briefly. It was so bad it was funny. Almost. After viewing my tawdry scene (which took place in the basement, of course), one of my pals was inspired to say, "Ah, your secret shame." The experience also inspired a very successful segment in one of my stand-up comedy routines. That's the last joke of this chapter. Fasten your seatbelts.

I was wary of François from the get go. He was an interloper at a dinner where not only was he not invited, but the gal who invited him was not invited, either. I was suspicious of them both. They were hangers on. From Paris, no less. And I'm all for Paris. I'm just not for hangers on.

I was to dine alone with my English pal Martin, someone whose company I valued greatly, a compadre from the personal growth world. We'd spent a few weeks together in the woods for a wonderful class. I trusted him. I liked him. But he, alack, had fallen in love, sigh…with a beautiful French girl, Cerise, and he was beholden to her world. Cerise was not with him for this trip to New York. However, we were now saddled with two of her friends because Martin was courting them as surely as he was courting her.

The young man, François, was an artist. Rail thin. Très, très polite. Polished. Charmant. He reached out to me with his business card, and I reciprocated with mine. It turned out we shared a love of puppetry and metaphysics and I eventually invited him to a meditation/prayer/psychic development group I ran in my home. He was an astrologer, a drinker, and gay. He knew how to open a bottle of wine, how to pour it with panache, and with nary a drop spilled. When someone brought Moet to the group (we shared snacks and wine after the meeting) an uncouth character wanted to mix orange juice with his champagne.

François would not allow it. "Non! If you are going to mix the Moet you cannot have any. It's too good." Right on.

He was fairly psychic and very open to the energies of the group, which was mostly female. Wouldn't be the first time girls and gays got along well. I saw several psychic images for him involving the color red and velocity, like a fast sports car. I saw a tall red tulip and the Eiffel Tower. He seemed to comprehend the meaning of these images, though I did not. Psychic images are very often symbolic, like messages from the dream world. It takes time and patience to unravel the language of your subconscious. It's worth the effort, for you are mining your own gold when you do so. It is sometimes impossible to understand what these symbols mean for someone else.

François offered to give me a free astrological/numerological reading. I was touched and accepted, but somewhat creeped out when he actually gave it to me. I don't remember the specifics, only that I felt unsettled. Discomfited. A good reading is not meant to butter you up and play to your weaknesses, but it is certainly not intended to bring you down. What's the value in that?

I socialized with him from time to time, mostly at art events he invited me to. His friends were the loveliest of females. Artists, painters, gallery owners, psychics, mediums, costume designers. Every gal he brought to my group was a gem. Warm, sweet, loving, and somewhat vulnerable. I loved each and every one.

He took photos of my dog when I needed them, and he and I and one other guy and gal enjoyed a lovely outing at Coney Island, inspired by a vision I'd had for the gal, a close friend of François. It was an easy, breezy day with the Frenchman and his male friend, a chef at a European embassy, and a real pleasure to be with such polite and charming guys. The other gal was François' good friend Agata, a shy, sweet artist, also foreign, and very "sensitive," with almost no English skills. François spoke with her in her native tongue. I was quite fond of her.

Through the various metaphysical classes and workshops I've taken over the years I've made lots of friends, including Sonia, who I met while studying mediumship with James Van Praagh. Brazilian, she was the life of the party, wild, crazy, mediumistic, a massage therapist, and healer. Sonia was up from Miami working in New York for a few days. She called me when her free housing in the city ended. I put her up. She gave me a wonderful massage.

Sonia participated in my development circle and while François was not there, his costume designer friend Celeste (also French) was. Sonia focused on Celeste. She uttered François' name (even though she'd never met him) then said she felt "Dark energy and sickness...I see a hermaphrodite...Black and white tiles... Danger...A masked man with a cape, like Zorro."

Celeste stated definitively, "This message is not for me."

I thought it was, including the fact that her friend's name had been specified. Turns out Celeste was right. The reading was for François.

After everyone left Sonia confided in me. "Valerie. I was terrified. Petrified of what I saw. There was Death, Valerie, Death. It was awful. There was something very, *very* dark and deadly. I can feel it now."

Sonia couldn't explain more but I could see how shaken she was. Eventually I decided to share this message with François. I became convinced that I knew what it meant. The darkness, the danger, the death, came from his Moroccan friend Maria (who I wrote about in "The Gypsy Curse"). She was a "hermaphrodite" (yes, I'm pushing the meaning of bisexual) having put her hand on my thigh under the table during a dinner out. She had a rich French boyfriend, and was now pregnant by him.

Maria's Parisian friend Celeste was involved with my English friend Martin (also rich). The potential for use and abuse was there. François was not rich. But he worshipped Maria, the gypsy, whom I'd met and been read by. He believed in her powers, vision, and ability. I was very careful how I couched all of this with François. Maria was his best friend. I was accusing her, essentially, of being involved in the black arts, which would explain the death and darkness that Sonia psychically perceived. What was Sonia picking up on? I don't know. But she looked like she'd just sat through *The Silence of the Lambs*.

I made it clear to François that I thought his friend could be dangerous. He was disturbed by the warning, but eventually decided that he could interpret the black and white tile "message" for himself, because Maria's sister, also a witchy type, had given him black and white substances to create magic spells with. So, now the black magic accusation was getting pawned off onto Maria's sister. Mind you, I'm not putting down Wicca and Pagan beliefs and practices that are of the Light. Glenda the Good was a Good Witch. But this magic was of questionable nature. He was told to use it in his place of work, run by the nicest gallery owner (whom I'd met) a woman who had consistently helped François with green card issues. What was the spell to accomplish? His response was vague.

Referring to the black and white "substances," I said, "Get rid of them."

He asked me how he should throw them out.

I said, "It doesn't matter how! Just get them out of your house, whatever they are."

He told me he threw them out the next day.

Now, for sure, François had some interesting habits. During my meetings, which lasted 2-4 hours, he would disappear twice for ten to twenty minutes at a pop, off into the bathroom. Now, a girl does this, one generally doesn't blink. But a boy? Repeatedly? One starts to question gastrointestinal issues. When this happens week after week, one just starts to wonder. Yes, I keep lovely reading material in the bathroom, my favorite channeled periodical, *The Sedona Journal of Emergence*. That was one plausible explanation. He mentioned looking at it once. But it didn't explain two visits to the loo for ten to twenty minutes each meeting. This was inexplicable, not to mention rude, behavior.

Being a rather blunt person, I finally blurted out one day after yet another one of his lengthy excursions to the toilet, "What the heck are you doing in there?"

"Oh, I was putting lotion on my skin, it was very dry from the beach." He'd said he was at the beach that day. Okay. So what about every other day? He didn't go to the beach every week. It was a facile lie.

Since I knew he was preoccupied with sex (he felt that explained all my red, hot psychic imagery for him) I wondered if he was jerking off in the bathroom. Nice. Not what I invite people into my home for, especially not for spiritual development. No sir. During the group he talked about men he picked up, and since we prayed and meditated for ourselves and others, he asked us to pray for a violent guy he'd picked up who was now stalking him.

"No," I said. "We're not going to pray for him. We're going to pray for *you*. Because you attracted him. It's your problem, not his."

He asked us to pray for his frail grandmother in France who was being robbed blind by her young aide who, inexplicably, the family refused to fire. We prayed repeatedly for Grand-Mère's protection and well-being. François remained just pleasant, charming, and useful enough to remain on my good side until one night. His French friend Celeste came to the group and brought comté, a fine French gruyère. I was enthralled by the flavor, however being quite full I looked forward to enjoying my share of the comté the following day. There was a piece about one by three inches left on the table, perfect to accompany my lunch. We retired to the living room and that was that.

When François readied to leave he moved to clean the table, something he'd never done before.

I protested. "Please, no, don't do that,"

"I *insist*," he said.

"Thank you, but I *prefer* that you not. Please just leave everything where it is."

Going against my wishes he brought plates into my tiny, crowded kitchen. When he left, the cheese was gone. This may seem a petty thing, but it amounted to petty theft. It was my home, my table, my request that he do nothing, my cheese, and most importantly, my lunch. Don't fuck with my lunch. The cheese was not in the trash. It was not on the counter, nor in the fridge. He had taken it.

Now, if he had simply said, "I'm taking the cheese!" it wouldn't have been so bad.

I could have yelled, "Wait! I didn't have any tonight! I want it."

The fact that he *pretended* to be helpful in order to get what he wanted was disturbingly manipulative. I emailed him the next day. "I would have appreciated it if you'd just asked for the cheese and not pretended to clean up in order to take it."

He responded, "*Darling*! I don't know what you're talking about. Your cats ate it!"

He was digging himself into a deeper and deeper grave. My cats don't eat cheese. Never have. Not a one. I had one who ate peanut butter and chocolate (this was before I knew chocolate was dangerous for cats and dogs, but it never hurt him, and it only endeared him to me), one cat who drinks organic half and half with relish (if it is very, *very* fresh), but never a one, in 27 years, who ate cheese. Not even a speck of parmesan.

Now I was mad. He was accusing my cats of theft! How dare he? The ruse was just so, so absurd and all for a fraction of fromage. Seriously. The fact that he created drama and lies around such an innocuous event was disturbing. A mist of distrust swirled up within me.

Nonetheless, he asked to use my computer before a meeting, and I was more than happy to oblige him. My guard was down again. "If you ever want to sleep over," I offered. Why did I say that? He was poor, lived in Queens, worked in Manhattan, and I had an extra bed. I felt the desire to help him. Apparently, other women were compelled to mother and mentor him as well.

The friendship continued and the plot thickened. I went to a development circle with him in Connecticut, a group I'd attended regularly for a year. We did a "speed dating" type psychic exercise, where you line up in rows and read the person directly in front of you before moving briskly down the line. Everyone read six to eight people and got read by six to eight people. It's intense, loud, and fast. You have to stay on your toes.

A woman I did not know sensed my father's spirit. He held a baby in his arms. "Were you the baby of the family?"

"Yes."

"That, or he's just calling you his baby."

Either one worked for me.

"Your father doesn't like the man who was just in your house."

I was confused, as I often was by psychic messages. Some of them you have to think about. They must marinate before the meaning kicks in. Some of them don't make sense 'til months or years later. Some of them never make sense. At any rate, you say "thank you" to the person offering the message and leave it at that.

I took the train home with François and shared the message with him. I said, "It makes no sense because the only man who was in my home last night was you. But you're my friend." I had held a circle the previous night.

François coyly said, "I *hope* he does not mean me!"

I hugged him. "Of course not! How could he?" But what *did* my father mean?

Something else the woman said stuck in my head. "Are you missing something? Something under the sink, in the kitchen?"

Now I started to wonder what could be missing and who could have taken it. I trusted the staff in my building, really trusted them. Good guys, good men. They had the keys to my apartment. They'd also worked under my kitchen sink recently. What the hell would they have taken, a can of Pledge? Because my suspicions had been raised I was now racing through my mind…in whom have I mistakenly placed trust? It's a creepy thought when you contemplate not really knowing the people you think you know. I found nothing missing.

When I stepped out of the shower the next morning I looked for my moisturizer. My body lotion, under the *bathroom* sink, was gone. Not just any body lotion, but special cream from Bliss, Lemon and Sage shea butter. Pricey stuff, something I'd just splurged on. I felt sick. So it wasn't missing from the kitchen. She'd picked up "under the sink." Close enough. Body lotion indeed. He'd already admitted to using it in my bathroom (during his extended stay there) when his skin was dry "from the beach."

Now a brand new tube was gone. Stealing from a friend is pretty crappy. First the cheese, now the cream? My head was spinning with the implications. If he commits these petty acts and lies about them so easily, what else is he doing? I asked a psychic friend of mine to focus on him. I've referred to her before. She's razor sharp, whip smart, and has laser beam accuracy. It was a few weeks before I saw her and she was able to focus on him.

"Who's David?"

"I have no idea"

"Why am I seeing Lincoln Center?"

"Beats me."

"Does he have ties to Spain?"

"Yes"

"I'm seeing the Camino de Santiago Campostela"

"His Spanish friend just walked it."

Damn, she was good. She didn't know these people.

"Is he a transvestite?"

This made me gulp, hard. He got a psychic reading from someone in my group who saw a false eyelash drop into a bowl of soup. He laughed and said it had happened to him when he was on a date with someone, someone he didn't know was a transvestite. How is that possible if your gay date is wearing false eyelashes? The pieces fell together. The lady doth protest too much. He was the transvestite. His mannerisms, delicacy, and rail thinness would only contribute to his skills in that department.

And then my friend froze. She stiffened. "Oh God, why do they show me this stuff?"

"What?" I said both wanting and not wanting to know.

"Do you feel safe with him?"

My blood curdled.

"I did until now…Why?"

"I'm picking up violence. It's ugly. I think he has the ability to rape. You. Drugs. He would drug you first."

Okay. Stop right there. The guy's *gay*. He's gay! He's a 90-pound weakling and looks like a marionette! Why would he *want* to have sex with me, for God's sake, let alone *rape* me? It was crazy.

But then more memories kicked in, chilling my blood further. He had admitted in my group (casually, I might add) that he'd been accused of raping a girl when he was *thirteen*. Rather young, but more surprisingly, why would he be with a girl?

"Oh, I've slept with girls," he said.

"What? Why?" I was utterly perplexed. This guy was way gay.

"I had sex with that twelve year old girl, but it was consensual. We were friends."

It seems there was a rather ugly fight between their two families. But the fact that he'd even had sex with a girl, let alone a twelve year-old girl, was shocking to me. Rape? Sex addict. Liar. Thief. Still, he remained charming, and in my life.

He drank up a storm. He was a bottomless well, and never showed alcohol's effects. He confessed he'd raised the eyebrows of his costume designer friend, Celeste. She and her husband had him to their New Year's Eve party. She questioned his sobriety. "What is wrong with you?" she grilled.

He responded, "Oh, someone must have slipped something in my drink."

So, you use drugs, too. Fine. *Don't lie about it.* The eyelashes, the drugs, they were always "somebody else's." Are you getting the picture?

So now my psychic friend tells me François has the capacity (and the desire) to drug and rape me? It was utterly mind boggling. None of this is provable, but the evidence was mounting; the adolescent rape accusation, the known abuse of sex, alcohol, and drugs. *The cheese.* Besmirching my cats' good reputations. How low could he go? And did I want to stick around to find out?

Not long after this, my psychic friend had a nightmare about him. She saw a meditation group and all the girls were wearing yellow (this is a symbol of intuitive ability). Sounded like my group. He was there. And when she saw him she heard the words "serial killer."

Now *profoundly* concerned, I ran him by another "sensitive" friend who had met him at my group. She confessed that she thought he was terrible, dangerous, and horrible. I was shocked and upset. "Why didn't you tell me?!"

"Because he was your friend," she replied.

"Um, hello! All the more reason to tell me, I trust you! Please, *please* tell me if you pick up any stuff like this in the future. I don't want dark energies or people in my home or life."

It seemed when he was doing his friendly astrology/numerology schtick in the group, he'd asked this girl not only what her birthdate was, but the *exact* spelling of her name, for "numerological purposes." I was there and heard the question, I watched him as he wrote it all down on paper and pen he'd borrowed from me. Nothing unusual about that. But when she went to get her purse that evening, she felt his energy all over it. She psychically saw him rifling through her bag and her wallet. A chill went through her. The two of them ended up leaving at the same time, and they waited for the elevator together. She looked right through him. He shot her a murderous look back. She was so disturbed she got on the phone that night and cancelled all her credit cards. She felt he was involved in an identity theft ring. I knew he was desperately trying to obtain his work visa/green card.

Now the original warning from Sonia made sense. The hermaphrodite. Sure, it could apply to his crazy gypsy friend who put her hand on my thigh, but François was "both man and woman," too. The caped, masked figure. Who is he? I don't know. I don't want to know.

"Death, Valerie, I saw Death. I smelled it. I felt it. It was terrible." This from psychic number one, and months later, from another, "rape, drugs, serial killer." Both people who don't know him. Not good status reports.

I went from thinking he was jerking off in my bathroom to trying to crack my computer and banking codes. He had a smart phone. He was smart. I will never know for sure what he was doing. I just know he wasn't putting "lotion on his skin." And was it the home aide in France robbing his frail old grandmother blind, or was it him or one of his friends? Criminals have the oddest way of confessing their sins…

What do I conclude? That it's no accident that his female friends were warm, loving, and vulnerable (except for his gypsy pal). I believe he used their energy somehow, like a psychic vampire. Every one of his girl friends also had funds (except his gypsy pal). He was obsessed with lower energies: sex, drugs, and alcohol.

I knew a gal who went to a Santeria ritual (or two). This was a savvy, sassy New York businesswoman from California. She did not suffer fools gladly. But in this Santeria ritual she was told to lie on the floor and spread her legs (she was clothed).

"You did it?" I asked, appalled. She nodded. "Why'd you do it?"

She shrugged, but admitted she didn't feel comfortable there and never went back. I'm not well versed in the dark arts but I know enough to know that people and their energy can be used by psychic or "energy" vampires. Darkness can feed off of light. And for a woman to spread her legs at a ritual run by men…were they sucking energy out or putting it in? I have no idea. But you wouldn't catch me there…No religion that hurts animals and takes life is of the Light. God doesn't need sacrifice. God *has* everything, *is* everything, *creates* everything. How could killing His/Her innocent children possibly be a sign of allegiance?

François confessed to me. "I want you to know I finally threw that black and white stuff out."

"I know you did, you told me that months ago."

"No, I didn't. I just said that to make you feel better. I threw it out last night." He kept admitting his lies. And he kept lying.

When I decided to eject him from my bathroom (and my life) I emailed one of his dear friends who came to my group. "I want you to know that I'm not speaking to François right now, but you are more than welcome to come to the meeting." She contacted him immediately, and he, in turn, confronted me. I did not pick up the phone. He called repeatedly and left several messages. He was hopping mad.

I wrote him an email. "I know this may seem confusing to you, as it does to me, but I must consider the meaning of my father's message. Thank you for your understanding." No need to tick off an identity/cheese thief, hermaphrodite serial killer. But if he was a real friend, wouldn't he be hurt or confused by my rejection? Why angry? There was no pleading on his part or trying to understand my position, no apology of any kind, even if he didn't know what to apologize for. He was simply livid.

I know all of this sounds crazy, and it is, but I share it as an example of how important it is to take stock of your feelings, inconsistencies in people's behavior, and the integrity of the people around you. Has this person committed violent crimes? I have no way of knowing.

Here's what I think…because he is an addict and therefore keeps his spiritual vibration low (drugs, sex, alcohol, lies, stealing) he is vulnerable to being *used* by powerful, dark energies. Perhaps that is the masked, caped figure, a dark violent force that feeds off of him, like a psychic vampire. Creepy. And what's creepier yet is how much I enjoyed his company, and for so long (around two years, I'd say). He remained my "charming French friend."

A year or more later he reached out to me via Facebook saying, "I take your recent FB connection with one of my friends as a positive sign for us. I'm not angry. I just miss you and want to be friends again. As you know, I am very blunt, like you, and *honest*…"

I could hear the H as he pronounced "honest" (like honey), with his French accent. Ask a liar if he's telling you the truth, and he'll say yes, even as the cheese lies in his belly. "Come closer, little girl," said the big bad wolf in grandma's bed.

CHAPTER 20

"HOW MANY GLASSES OF WINE?"

January 8, 2012

"How many glasses of wine do you have to drink before you wrap your legs around me again?" he asked. It had been several weeks since we first met, a night that started with fireworks and crescendoed with...well, I'll get to that part later.

I was intoxicated when I met him. With good food and wine initially, and additionally by the fact of meeting him. He was someone I had admired from afar for years, and when I met him, quite by surprise...the thrill of this chance encounter heightened my buzz. The fact that he liked me added fuel to the warmth of the restaurant, the meal, the night.

I was dining with friends at a restaurant near their country home. The restaurant was cosy and charming. I was very happy. I was on my way to a personal growth class in the country, a place I had blossomed at over many visits. I hadn't been there in five years and was excited to return.

I was eating mussels and salad when the waitress came over and told us the name of this gentleman, said he was sitting "right over there."

I jumped in my seat. "Where? Where?!"

She pointed and I spotted him. Yes, that was him! I knew what he looked like. I had seen him on TV and thought he was aging well, thought that he was very handsome. He saw me looking and smiled at me. My friends were confused, not really sure who he was. I quickly filled them in and told them I would be assaulting him shortly. I'm not an autograph hound, but when I truly admire someone, I quickly and discreetly let him or her know.

He was with two male friends and I didn't want to disturb them, so I surveyed their conversation to determine when it would be appropriate for me to interrupt. As I continued to look over he continued to look back and smiled at me each time. I whispered to my friend, "He's smiling at me."

When the time was right I approached his table and confirmed his identity. " I love your story." I said. "I love what you did." He thanked me. His friends invited me to join them. They were gracious and engaged me in conversation.

After five minutes one guy said, "Well, buddy, happy birthday. Good night." His friends left.

"Happy birthday," I said awkwardly. Pause. We were alone now. I asked if he'd like to join my table, where we were finishing dinner. He obliged.

I was already drunk, a good three glasses of red down the hatch, which for me, is a titanic quantity. I was woozy on wine and being with this man. Meeting him was electrifying. He had sparkling eyes and a vibrant personality. I was buzzing. We rubbed elbows at the table. Our knees touched below. We were like giddy teenagers. My friends watched, not sure what to think.

When we finished dinner my friend's husband told him we were going to the local pub, would he like to join us? He nodded. He trailed beside me like a puppy dog, occasionally stopping to flirt with local girls, but it didn't bother me. I knew he was with me. He told me later that evening he'd been accused of being a womanizer. The man was like the mayor. Everybody in town knew and greeted him. I told him he was a "peopleizer."

At the pub, he vivaciously regaled us with tales from his famous life. It was story time around the campfire. Our knees and elbows continued to touch. The band was loud so my friend's husband said, "We're going home to open a bottle of wine. Would you like to join us?"

He nodded. It was terribly surreal. We were all on a ride to God knows where with this guy.

My friend's husband gave him driving directions. I turned to leave with my friends, but they had vanished. All of a sudden, I was in his sports car. If I had been in a horse and buggy with Abraham Lincoln I couldn't have been more surprised. A fire was blazing in the living room when we arrived at the house. The bottle was opened and we sipped a little to be polite. Drink had played all the role it could that night. I put my feet in his lap and he gave me a foot rub. A rough one. He had some reflexology training and it hurt. My friend and her husband looked on, amazed at the two of us. He was twenty-seven years my senior. Her husband said, "Well, we're going to bed, guy. My house is your house." And they went upstairs.

We continued to touch and talk. We tried on each other's rings. He was handsome, but he was *old*. I'd never been with anyone chronologically older than 38. This man was 69. Or was it seventy? I kept trying to do the math based on what I knew about him, and between the wine and the hope that he was only in his sixties, I concluded that he was 69. Seventy was just too fuckin' *old*. The skin on his neck was loose. I looked at his mouth and had no desire to kiss it. We held each other but didn't lock lips.

I told him my parents had died when I was relatively young.

"Oh, a little orphan," he said and sang a few lines of Italian opera to me. "Do you know what that means?" I shook my head. "Daddy's little girl."

He stroked my hair. Some of my friends thought that was creepy. I didn't. Dad died when I was five, and I'd only been with younger, selfish, irresponsible guys. My guard went down. I was mesmerized.

We lay down, my head on his chest. It was hard. Bony. He was trim, but not buff. I did my best to work with what was there but was not turned on by it. On the other hand, I liked him and I was drunk. I knew I could sleep with this guy and what a story that would make. What a crazy anecdote. But I also knew that I couldn't predict what I would be getting into. No one is just an anecdote. There's a person there. This guy was a wild card, an unidentified can of worms. I was playing with fire.

My eyes closed, my body on his body, I surrendered to the woozy feelings of wine and attraction, while the caveats swirled around my head. I refused to deal with his face and neck, so I focused on the body. I ran my hand up his chest, sought out the flesh beneath his shirt, and recoiled. The skin was soft and loose. I stroked his chest briefly then withdrew to the safety above fabric. His hand reached down to touch the top of my ass, under my jeans. He touched my breast, above my shirt. My eyes remained closed. This was a dream. But the reality was that my legs were on top of his thighs, and I couldn't feel any hardness between them. I had been with a younger lover not too long before who had difficulties in this area, and the thought of dealing with that scenario again, not to mention with an older, non-functioning model, was not something I could cope with. I was missing the heat and hardness of a man who is aroused. He wasn't ready. We were going through the motions. I ran up the white flag and fell asleep on his chest.

In the morning my friend's husband was nonchalant. "How did you sleep?"

"Well."

"What happened with him?"

"We slept together."

He went nuts. "What?! NO!!! You *didn't!*"

Even though this guy had totally pimped me out the night before he was *shocked* that I would actually go through with it.

"I didn't have sex with him," I said. "We fell asleep. I kicked him out at 3:30 when I woke up."

He breathed a sigh of relief.

But my gentleman caller called that morning and joined us outdoors for a picnic and kayaking. He did all the talking and ranted ad infinitum, reading from a play he'd written. By the end of the afternoon I was thoroughly fed up with this fellow, decided he was a wack job, and let my friends know that I was done. We bid him adieu and he kissed my hand chivalrously, even though I'd been very dismissive of him that day.

So an anecdote he became. He was the old guy I snuggled with. Weeks went by and we spoke on the phone. He asked me when I was coming his way again, and I told him I didn't know, but that I would tell him when I did. When I visited my friends' country home again I didn't call him. We went out to lunch Saturday. There he was, at the restaurant. My first instinct was to duck and hide, but I swiftly decided to stand right in front of him. He looked amazed then took me in his arms. He joined us for lunch.

He was jocular, "on," in his peopleizer mode, mayor of the town. I invited him to my friend Mark's restaurant opening that night. Conan O' Brien would be there. Mark and I went to college with him.

At the celebration we were flirty and relaxed. There was no denying we liked each other. He worked the room but always circled back to me. He cornered me at the bar, me with a bellini, he with a glass of red.

"So. How many glasses of wine do you need before you wrap your legs around me again?"

I looked away and laughed the question off. I continued the conversation by asking him questions, and remarked that he knew nothing about me.

He said, "I figured if there was something you wanted me to know, you would tell me."

I said, "You could ask me questions." He never did.

I flirted with everyone that night, with Mark's utterly adorable dad, a grandfather who reminded me of Vincent Gardenia. I flirted with Mark's brother, also married with kids. I was having such a grand time, I chose to skip my ride back with my hosts. I had ride offers from Mark *and* his brother. By the time I was ready to leave, my gentleman caller put in a third bid. I decided to go with him.

He drove me around Main Street trying to impress me, it seemed, with how fabulous this little town was. He explained every restaurant and bar to me. Took me down to the river. I decided to divulge something very personal about myself, something meaningful to me. He interrupted me mid-*sentence*. It was obvious he didn't want to know anything about me. It was all about him. This turned me off considerably, as did the bleak, weighty Italian peasant music he put on.

I couldn't wait to get out of his car, out of this situation. Given what happened the last time he was here I warned him, "If my friends are up when we arrive, you can come over for a little bit. But if they're not, I'm going to bed." The lights were off when we arrived. He would not be coming in. He walked me to the door and kissed me on the lips, but no tongue, thank God.

He said, "Ciao, bambina."

I kissed him on the neck I had been avoiding. The dreaded neck and lips had been broached, but I wasn't wanting more. I retreated to the safety of my bedroom, alone in my friends' house.

I returned to New York City to resume mooning over my last lover and to fuck a new one. My last lover was a 38-year-old manic-depressive pothead who washed down lithium and other assorted prescription pills daily with blue Gatorade. There were positive qualities which recommended this fellow, but overall the casual relationship I had with him was an emotional rollercoaster for me.

I said to him once, "I'm not looking for commitment, just *consistency*."

This was before I discovered he was manic depressive. He would appear and disappear, emotionally and physically, creating *just* enough tension in my life for me to lose weight and weep constantly. It was a winning combination. My friends called him my "science project" and urged me to break up with him.

I said, "I'll think about it in another five pounds."

It was also what prompted me to go back to my personal growth place in the woods and get on a positive track. It was here that I met a robust 28-year-old who took an immediate fancy to me.

Well, he wasn't so robust, it turned out. Despite his youth and large frame, he had a few problems. More than a few, actually. After being abandoned as a baby, his adoptive mom died of cancer when he was 19. His adoptive dad, a physician, killed himself a year later. Brian became a fireman and EMS medic and married his childhood sweetheart when they were eighteen and had a daughter with her. After 9/11, he left Dallas for three weeks to help out at Ground Zero in downtown New York. The following New Year's Eve in Dallas, he was the first medic on the scene of a car crash resulting from a drunk-driving incident. His wife and daughter were the victims. They both died.

I had never heard of more disaster from one person. I didn't feel sorry for him, and I think that's why he liked me so much. I was just amazed. And there was yet more drama, there were the slashed wrists, the narcotics anonymous pendant hanging from his neck, not to mention his totally annoying habit of mooching off of everybody in the group. This guy was Drama Central. But the kicker, the reason he was at this joint with me, taking a class to learn how to be happier, was he had been diagnosed with pancreatic cancer and had six to twelve months to live. Despite the pathos, and despite his desperate desire to be close to me physically, I kept him at bay the week we were in class. Bottom line was: this crass, chain-smoking, beer-drinking Yankees fan just wasn't my type.

I had such a great time in this class, I was thrilled to hear from two of my classmates when I returned to New York. One was a South American girl with an English accent who lived in Europe. She had been my roommate during the program, and I had avoided her all week at all costs. A beautiful but strange girl who showered in the middle of the night and drank green stuff for breakfast, I saw no need to bond with her despite her repeated requests to walk and talk with me. I thought she was a weird hippie, and there were others with whom I preferred to spend my time. But without others to compete for my attention in New York, I was happy to house her for one night while she was en route back home. We were thick as thieves for 24 hours. The woman I had assiduously ignored for five days adored the same books and ideas that I did and one conversation flowed exuberantly into the next. We had to force ourselves to go to sleep.

On the day Gabriella was leaving, I received a call from Brian, the dying, beer-swilling dude. I was thrilled to hear from him, too. I'd had such a good time with Gabriella, someone I'd found distasteful in the woods but delightful in my home, I decided to embrace Brian and accept his invitation to attend a (gag) Yankees game. I'd been once before, decades past, and recall enjoying the hot dog but noting that I didn't require four hours to eat it. Despite my lack of interest in Brian, it wasn't *terrible* that he was young, attracted, and paying attention to me. What was terrible was that he brought his *girlfriend* with him, an adoring little blonde. He paid attention to both of us, skewed in my favor. Being a simple girl, she accepted his explanation that I was just a friend, and while that's what I was, that's not what he wanted me to be. I had no idea he had a girlfriend. Despite their hand holding and her adoring stares, he told me he was just staying with her and that she was just a big tease. It didn't stop him from hitting her up for cash at the ticket counter. I paid for nothing. No way in hell I'm spending my money on boys playing with balls.

The best part of the game was we had good seats, and I thought the lawn was pretty. It was mowed in a lovely plaid motif and I thought it would make a nice carpet. I stared at the green of the grass and the blue of the sky. I like bright colors. What they were doing with that little white ball I had no idea. However, without a hot dog this time, the four hours loomed even longer, and frozen to the bone, I cut out after just two hours. Despite his love of the sport, Brian trailed after me, and Suzie trailed after him. We took the subway back from the Bronx, and I left them to their hand-holding.

The next time I saw Brian he left Goldilocks at home. He picked me up at my gym. He got all dressed up (for him) and bought me enough margaritas to change my mind about sports. By the time the buzz wore off, I remembered my hatred of sports but felt obligated to go through with what had developed over the evening, an increasing intimacy and eroticism which implied fulfillment. Despite my growing reticence, I chalked up my decision to go through with it to the fact that hey, the guy was dying. I put on my nurse's uniform and proceeded with the mercy fuck.

The act itself was unmemorable other than the fact that I still remember it. He was tall and large, in the other sense about which he was quite proud, but didn't impress me since I'm so small. When he wanted to go again in the morning, I balked.

I said, "Put that thing away. It's a weapon. What are you trying to do, kill me?"

I do like a good workout, however, and I met him once more. This time he was not feeling well. He was in pain and needed ibuprofin since he was out of his normal painkiller for the cancer. I asked what he took. He said Dilaudid and I froze. Not only did my mom take Dilaudid, but she died from pancreatic cancer. The evening took on a maudlin, and eventually weepy tone for me. Here I was physically close to someone dying of pancreatic cancer. Again. Everything started hitting me hard. I teared up.

I don't remember the sex clearly. I remember wetting his shirt with my tears. He asked what was wrong and I couldn't tell him, "Well, your dying of the same thing my mom died of makes me really sad." I whispered, "Just feeling emotional."

He accepted my answer and left, running off to his next social engagement. The guy was living the end of his life to the fullest, eating, drinking, carousing, traveling, blowing money left right and center. He was going out with a bang. And I was descending into my own underworld of sex, death, love, and longing.

CHAPTER 21

LOVE LIKE THE SUN

January 18, 2012

My parents had my sister Diane in the 1950s. Despite feeling thrilled and blessed to have her, they wanted more kids but none came. My sister begged my mom for a little sister or brother to no avail. One day my sister came back from a friend's house and confessed that she was relieved not to have one. My mother was curious about the change of heart. Turns out the friend's little brother had been a royal pain in the ass that morning. Son of a bitch, this was the very day my mother was going to announce her pregnancy with me to Diane. Despite this uncanny glitch, my sister came around quickly enough. There are nine years between us.

I come from a line of untraditional but deeply spiritual people. While there was orthodoxy on both sides (Greek and Jewish) both religions had been rejected by A) my Greek mother and B) my father's German Jewish parents. I was raised a Theosophist, a Western philosophy based on Eastern religion. No one drank. No one cursed. We were a squeaky clean family, parked in the middle of New York City.

Then disaster struck. While we were at Sunday school we were informed that my dad had been killed in a plane accident. My father, a WWII pilot with the Army Air Corps., was Jimmy Stewart's lead navigator in the European theater. He was simulating WWII dogfights with another pilot at an air show in Canada in original WWII planes when their maneuvers resulted in my father's death. It was 1968. I was five. Dad was 47. Mom was 47. She never dated again. He was the love of her life and a man of such exceptional caliber that she said, "If I met a man half as special as your father, I would consider remarrying." She never did, so I grew up without a dad.

Mom soldiered on. Her Greek name was Ismine but she went by Nina, and pronounced it *Neye*-na, not *Nee*-na. She was strong, an American born Greek, and had already lived through several tragedies (though she never complained about them), including growing up during the Depression. Not that the Depression was a tragedy. But it had its challenges. Nonetheless my mother said they always felt rich because they had each other. And no one around them had any more than they did. Her father, Christos, worked in a metal plating plant and used to come home on payday and, with great fanfare, drop dollar bills on the ground one by one as if they were chump change, that's how rich they were!

Christos got cancer while my mom was in college. It was WWII and her big brother Pete was doing his part in the Army's Pacific Theater. Her dad could no longer work. Mom, a strong and enthusiastic English student, dropped out to support her parents.

Years later, she was eight months pregnant with me when her mother, Iphigenia, with whom she was close, also died of cancer. She was giving life and losing it simultaneously—the greatest joy and the greatest sorrow, all in the same sandwich. I've recently started mulling over the fact that her amniotic fluid was steeped with sorrow and I marinated in it. I believe it eventually doubled with my own pain as I started accruing my own losses. Eventually, my grief became like a rumbling, massive black hole that threatened to suck in my light and life altogether.

I asked Mom years later how she felt losing her mom when she was about to have a baby.

She said, "It was hard. But you just go on."

They didn't think about stuff like "how they felt" back in the old days. They didn't analyze everything. She said the same damn thing about the bomb when I asked her what she and Dad thought about it. She said, "We never discussed it."

I was like, "You didn't DISCUSS it? What DID you talk about? Lunch?"

She ended the conversation by saying, "It ended the war."

Mom internalized most of her stress and took the rest out on me since my sister Diane was off to college four short years after my father's death. Mom and I were tight. We were so close that one of my high school teachers remarked at a reunion, "You guys were unique. You were a team."

Her familiarity with loss didn't make it any easier to take the sudden death of my father. In fact, it sucker punched her, amplifying the pains of the past, like an escalating, emotional clatter, a sorrow-filled sonic boom. She was shell-shocked and didn't know it. Mom was fiercely protective of me, and she challenged me to champion myself, too, which was embarrassing at times. I wasn't more than seven when Mom gave me money to go downstairs and get an ice cream cone on the corner of Lexington Avenue at Howard Johnsons. I got a scoop of peach. The ice cream plopped off of my cone within two licks. I trudged upstairs, crestfallen. Mom marched me back downstairs and told me to ask them for a new one. She made me do my own dirty work. I was totally appalled by what she wanted me to do, but lo and behold, they gave me another peach ice cream cone. And now I'm a self-confident, pushy broad who advocates for herself.

She taught me the value of speaking up. "Nothing ventured, nothing gained," she always said.

We were decidedly on a budget, living in a rent-controlled apartment. I went to public school, but Mom invested in me by springing for piano and dance lessons, summer camp, and acting class. I rarely got an allowance so I had to petition for things I dearly wanted. Most of them I never got (dog, cat, hamster, pinball machine, soda fountain, air hockey, horse). When I switched over to private school in seventh grade mom bought me knockoffs of the brands the rich girls were wearing. When one of the girls made fun of my fake Wallabees, I was pissed, not embarrassed. Mom gave me everything she could. We were on a First, not Park Avenue, budget.

When a large bank bought our tenement to tear it down and build their massive worldwide headquarters, we were evicted from the apartment. They offered Mom $1,000 to move. She was livid. The building was filled with little old ladies living alone on fixed incomes. There was Sarah, frail both physically and mentally. She had frightened eyes, wore her hair in ringlets, and had a pretty doll with hair in ringlets, too. I couldn't understand why she didn't just give the doll to me. I was the *kid*, after all. Now that I'm an adult with a fabulous toy collection of my own (I'm more of an Ugly Doll fan), I understand. We give ourselves what we missed out on as a child. I have a dog. And a cat. I could still go for the pinball machine, air hockey, horse, and you can substitute a ping pong table for the soda fountain since I've backed off of ice cream).

Across the hall and downstairs was Gaye, a bold, redheaded singer/storyteller with a record to her credit and a brilliant parrot who loved the "CH" sound. He chirped,

"Gaye go bye-bye CHurCHHHHHH. Ah CH CH CH CHOO, I love you." I loved visiting them.

Mom and I visited neighbor Sarah Arms once in her new apartment, years after the move. She had Collier's Syndrome. Her apartment was filled from floor to ceiling with newspaper. We had to slip through a maze of tiny alleys between the piles of neatly stacked newsprint. Sarah's eyes were even more frightened now; the doll was still there in her bedroom. When Mom and I departed, appalled, stunned, we left a trail of chalk white footprints in the hallway behind us from the dust in her apartment.

As a very sad postscript, I received a strange call decades ago from a social worker looking for my mother. There was a fire in Sarah's apartment, and she was badly, badly burned. Sarah had listed my mother, someone she hadn't seen in years, as her next of kin.

This "big bank" offered the little old ladies the same thousand dollars. They all took it. Mom was furious on their behalves. What would they do with a thousand dollars? Where would they go? How would they survive and for how long? My mother was indignant and refused their offer. She held out for more. And continued to hold out. Eventually, Mom was the only tenant left in the building (I was at camp, my sister was at college). The big bank used harassment tactics, removing the lock on the front door of the building so there was no security. Bums slept in the lobby. The bank finally coughed up $25,000 in 1971, which put my sister through MIT. They hadn't expected a fierce battle from a five-foot tall widow with bottle thick eyeglasses.

Growing up, my biggest fear was losing Mom. She was the only thing standing between me and the world. My sister was off living her life. My German grandparents were too old to take care of me. Mom constantly prepared me for her death, which increased my anxiety.

"If anything happens to me, this is where the papers are, the keys are here, here's who to call..." Mom was *too* vigilant, like the sun focused through a magnifying glass, breathing down my back, scrutinizing closely. She didn't want to lose me, either.

When I was fifteen my worst fear came true. Mom developed adult onset diabetes. It was the beginning of the end, and on some level, we both knew it. I learned to give her the twice-daily shots of insulin. I was loath to stick her with a needle at first, but we both got used to it, though it never stopped hurting her. She relied on me to break up the monotony and pain of sticking the needle in the same spots over and over when she was alone. Sickness and life and the fear of death were now inextricably tied.

She asked me to keep her company at her diabetes doctor's office one afternoon after school. He was a very pleasant Latin fellow with an accent, in his 30s or 40s. He had already seen my mother by the time I arrived.

"Can I draw your blood?" he asked simply (and rather seductively, I thought). He might as well have said, "suck," Dracula that he was.

I was compliant until laying into my mother later. "You tricked me!"

I was phobic about having my blood drawn and her pleas to get me tested heretofore had failed. She appealed to the Good Samaritan in me to accompany her. She was worried I had diabetes, too. I didn't.

I did not fall under the spell of a Latin man again until I saw Raul Julia play *Dracula* on Broadway. I was fifteen and he was, well, grownup.

"I never drink…wine," said the Count.

Sigh…I saw Raul first as a youngster. He starred in *Where's Charley* at the Circle in the Square Theatre and I thought, "This guy is *good!* This guy is *so good* he could be on *TV!*" Yes, he was. He was a fine actor and an even finer human being, involved with trying to solve world hunger. I saw him in one of his last performances before succumbing to stomach cancer at age 54. It was a reading at St. Thomas's Church on Fifth Avenue and 53rd Street in NYC (where Mariah Carey married Tommy Mottola).

He acknowledged his wife in the audience, and his son "Benjamin," pronouncing the J as H, and he solemnly nodded his head to his young child, who was only seven when his daddy finally died. In front of all those people, his fans, his audience, he took the time to acknowledge the ones he loved.

So, my family had the sweet tooth thing going on, is there *one* Greek person without it? Considering that no one drank, or did *anything*, frankly, besides read books and listen to classical music (that would be my German grandparents) sugar was the party going on in *our* house. Not all the time by any stretch, since "health food" was our default mode, but it was the devil, lurking. When Mom binged she went all out, having not one napoleon pastry (what is that, 1,000 calories?) but *two*. Not one candy bar, but three. Mom called it "sinning."

When I applied to colleges, Mom insisted I stay close-ish to home (no "California Dreaming" for me) so we had easier access to each other. This became increasingly vital when we learned my sophomore year that Mom now had pancreatic cancer too, which typically kills within six months. She remained a Trojan Woman and insisted I finish out my education at a top college and not transfer back to New York, which I wanted to do to stay close to her. When it came to it, she checked herself in and out of the hospital for surgery. She didn't want anyone to visit her. She was proud and fiercely independent. She was also terribly proud of me. I heard it mostly from her friends.

A minor medical issue arose for me. After having a *huge* cavity (so big that my doc called in other docs to gape at the cavern in my molar) filled by the school's dental clinic, it became clear that my wisdom teeth all needed pulling. I went through the school's medical services covered by my insurance. Turns out they would only do my teeth on an inpatient basis at the hospital, not the dental clinic, requiring general anesthesia and an overnight stay. I was still petrified of needles. My mom was into homeopathy and natural stuff and I was never inoculated. (I imagine there are plenty of kids petrified of needles because they *were* inoculated). The only needles I knew were from having blood drawn, and for some reason this was extremely painful for me. I could still "feel" the needle in my arm hours after.

I had a mandatory meeting with a young, cocky anesthesiologist in blue shower cap and booties who described what would happen to me. I had to sign the general anesthesia release (just in case I died) and I'd have to get an IV (a needle *left* in my body, totally *other* kind of needle horror) not to mention tubes down my throat so that I didn't drown in my own blood. He was describing a horror movie. This was *Marathon Man*.

"We'll give you a pill to relax, then we'll put you under."

I said, "What pill?"

"A sedative."

"Yes, but which one, Valium?"

He refused to answer, either that, or he patronizingly gave me the chemical descriptor so that I was left in the dark. I was angry. And scared. I exited the hospital in a daze, as if I was walking the plank. I walked the "green mile" back to my dorm room in the snow and blistering cold.

I called Mom and explained how frightened I was. How I didn't like the doctor, didn't want to get an IV, go under general, have tubes down my throat or stay overnight. I had *just* sorta gotten used to handling dentists. Growing up, Mom wouldn't let me get Novocain. She said the momentary pain of the drilling...*what* was she saying?! I can't even remember her argument because *there is none!* There's nothing worse than having a tooth drilled without Novocain (*Marathon Man, Marathon Man!*). That was *horrible*, and I had a fair number of cavities as a kid (Greek sweet tooth!). So there's a quick needle prick, some drooling, and weird numbness when you get the shot. (The one time I tried a tiny bit of cocaine, I felt like I was at the dentist, oh joy! I was edgy and numb. I don't understand that drug at all).

The only way my wisdom tooth extraction would be covered by insurance was to check me in overnight with that bastard in blue booties. Mom listened to my rant. She was up to her neck in school bills for me, and medical bills for her. I rarely missed a meal in the dining hall because they were already paid for. That's how we rolled. Get your money's worth.

She paused then said, "We'll do it in New York. We'll find someone to do it over the summer." I took a breath. I couldn't believe it. I didn't know what the answer was, only that dying young was the problem. I felt so relieved by her generous offer and so, so loved. She was in Calm Mom mode (not a constant by any means). There was Nervous Mom, Angry Mom, Critical Mom, Mean Mom, Distracted Mom. And there was Loving Mom. And there were many faces to Loving Mom: Playful, Silly, Generous, Understanding, and Profound. This decree from Loving Mom melted my worries like the sun melting snow. I felt expansive waves of relief and gratitude. The bone chilling cold of Boston disappeared. My fear and loneliness evaporated.

There was never a doubt that she was a fiercely devoted and protective mother. But for this moment she allowed her ever-present budget consciousness to be overshadowed by her desire to comfort me. "Don't worry, honey. Forget the hospital." She would pay out of pocket. I wouldn't have to be murdered by that smug prick at Health Services.

As a result, we had rather a delightful experience getting my wisdom teeth pulled. Mom found a guy on 57th Street. It seemed like a pretty cushy office, very patrician. I recall the bill being $500. To my mother's delight none other than Hermione Gingold (the champagne guzzling aunt in *Gigi*) was sitting in the large, softly lit, wood-paneled, waiting room. It was more like being at a cocktail party from the 1950s than a dental event.

I was advised to only get two teeth out at a time because it was so painful. "So painful? If it's that painful, I'll never come back! I want it over with *all at once*." Doing it two and two also meant double the recovery time. Doc agreed to do it my seemingly brutal and primitive way. I sat calmly in his procedure chair high above 57th Street. I directly faced a window and could see skyscrapers. It was so elegant, so New York, it was as if I were starring in a Cole Porter dental review. All that was absent were the cocktails. His assistant deftly inserted the needle in my forearm (I declined to watch) and the sodium pentothal hit my vein. There was no pain whatsoever. She told me to count backwards from ten. Big deal, I thought. By seven the skyscrapers were *melting*...Blackout. My mother ferried me home in a cab, and I went on Percodan immediately.

I looked pretty damn bad, like Mike Tyson had had his way with me (in the ring). My face blew up to the size of a basketball. I had black swollen slits for eyes. My skin was purple, blue and yellow. Mom approached my bed in the dark to put ice packs on my cheeks and the sound of the plastic bag (and I'm talking soft Baggies not loud crunchy plastic), containing the ice, *hurt my ears*. Everything was amplified. I was outright cranky to my mom, something I ordinarily wasn't.

"Go away! Go away!" I whimpered. There was swelling and a lot of pain for two weeks.

During my recuperation, I watched some TV, including a new daytime soap opera called *Texas*. I was never a soap fan. There was a fairly large contingent of *General Hospital* loyalists in my high school. I liked *All in the Family*, *Rhoda*, *Maude*, *Good Times*, and *Sanford and Son*. Oh, I liked *Dallas*, too. I guess that was a soap opera, wasn't it?

Well, I fell *in love* with *Texas*. I was on cloud nine watching it, and could not, *could not*, could *not* believe where I'd been without it! How could I have missed the sheer brilliance, the joy, the ecstasy, the *beauty* of that show? When I watched it again, not on Percodan, I realized what the problem was.

I revisited my mother's largesse just weeks ago when my darling cat Angela needed some dental work. I had *just* finished paying off her medical bills from six months prior.

Angela does not have medical insurance. Neither do I, for that matter. When my cat Wilbur had a cough it cost me $400 at *a clinic*, and they couldn't diagnosis the problem. They wanted to do a tracheal wash (sounds cheap, doesn't it?) or some shit, and an x-ray to check for pneumonia (I think I blew for that one). I don't remember the details. I stopped at $400 then took him to another doc for $150 when he seemed worse. I could have done more tests, I could have spent another $500 or more easily. They might have figured out what the problem was. They might not have. He died five days later at home. My diagnosis? Death.

So Angela's tooth was bleeding, of all things, and no, it wasn't her gums, even though she did have gingivitis. The middle of her tooth was bleeding when I brushed it. She's good about me brushing her teeth, but honestly, I don't brush 'em every day like you're supposed to. It was obvious she could use a dental cleaning. She had one three years ago and that was at least $300. Plus they have to put them under general anesthesia, which is a *big deal* (just ask the blue-bootied medical jerk from my college) and requires blood work, which means time, pain, and more money to see if the animal can "take" the general anesthesia.

So now I'm up against the crapshoot that going to a vet is. Will it be $400 or $1000? What are we looking at? The more you look, the more it costs, the more problems you find…It's unnerving, especially if you're on a budget. I started praying, "Oh please, just heal. Just heal!" I prayed to St. Francis (animal guy) and Archangel Raphael (healing guy). I gave Angela an herbal kitty formula for sore gums. It didn't work. The clock was ticking, my nerves were jangling, and my anxiety simmered.

I decided to trust my intuition, since I'm quite good at that now. There's a vet at my gym, a really nice gal who's generously offered free advice since Angela had her problems at the clinic last summer. She was so consistently kind and considerate, asking after Angela, even when we were not patients, that I determined to go to her office when I needed a vet, even though her fees are not inexpensive. But I'd been burned repeatedly by the clinic that *starts* with a lowball figure but ends up sky high by the time they're done nickel and diming you ("medical waste disposal fee"?) All those $2 and $300 add up.

I was still taking it one-day-at-a-time, watching Angela when Sally the vet came up to me in the gym. I was sitting in the lounge reading my beloved *Sedona Journal of Emergence* (an amazing channeled publication) while waiting for my class to begin.

Sally pulled my nose out of the magazine. "Class is starting, Val!"

I knew that this was a sign. It was a "Sally Alert" since I'd never been late and Sally had never retrieved me. I reached out to Sally after class and described Angela's situation. Sally thought she knew what it was and said calmly and sweetly that I should have it checked out.

I blurted, "Can you do it?"

"Sure, I can come in on Friday." (Which she normally doesn't do).

I called her office to book the appointment and asked if they could give me a clue as to cost. They said Sally would cover it with me over the phone.

Sally called that afternoon to discuss the situation. We were looking at an exam, a blood test, x-rays (kitty teeth are tricky!) probable extraction of the bloody tooth, and the possible extraction of other teeth. The estimate was high.

I said "Uh huh," while my life flashed before my eyes.

While I was on the phone with Sally, Angela jumped up on the bed I was standing near, looked up at me and started purring. Loudly. This was another sign. She was not only telling me that she needed help, but that Sally was the right person to give it.

A friend of mine heard the quote and said that I was crazy to agree to it and that I should haggle. This brought up all my fears and concerns. I didn't *want* to haggle, so I called my old clinic to compare their estimate. It started low, *but*, they insisted on doing the blood work *this* week, the results would come days later, then the surgery would be *next* week, and I *guarantee* you, by the time they were done, they would have hit Sally's quote. They lure you in with a lowball estimate just like those crappy moving companies, and then, when they hold your belongings (or cat) hostage, BAM, here's the *real* bill, sucker! Sally said she could do the blood work that morning, on the spot, have results within hours, and do the procedure in the afternoon.

It hit me that I was facing my mother's dilemma back in the day. Do I go "cheap" or do I take care of Angela's distress (and my own—*no* one likes two trips to the vet) by going with comfort, with warmth, and a friend? I decided not to worry about the cost, to just trust, flow, and do what I had to do. I was trusting God, Myself, Life, and my decision. If there's been one thing (and there have been many) I've learned since losing my job and health insurance nearly four years ago, it's that releasing fear and bravely embracing myself, new options, new ways of being, and *surrendering to surrender itself*, has been miraculous. I am in a far, far better place than I have ever been physically, emotionally, mentally, and spiritually.

Angela needed the dentistry, no question. A situation like this can lead to infection and death. It can also lead to not eating (a fate worse than death). On Thursday, my pal Fredda wrote me on Facebook, "How do you know Dr. Haddock?" (I had just friended Sally) "She's my Jezebel's doctor!" Jezebel is a very intelligent, witty and entertaining African Gray Parrot, and the apple of Fredda's eye. When Jezebel poops she says, "Mommy has to clean it up!" (Jezebel has her own FB page, btw).

This was more confirmation that I was going to the right person. I can't tell you how many different vets I've been to over the decades. It's always been exhausting, expensive, and quite often…sad.

Fredda booked an appointment with Sally contiguous to mine so we could all hang out, me, Fredda, Angela, and Jezebel. I hadn't seen Fredda in a while. A nightmare of sorts was now becoming a celebration. Fredda and Jezebel were waiting for us when Angela and I arrived Friday morning. Friends. Warmth. I smiled and sighed relief. Dr.

Haddock is a breath of fresh air, and she gave the most thorough, loving, happy, and gentle exam any of my pets has ever received. She even kissed Angela on the forehead. She took our photo, which later got posted on her practice's FB page. I was with family, not at a cold clinic. We were being loved. A giant man with a foreign accent came in and introduced himself.

"Don't worry. I'm not as scary as I look." He smiled.

More family. He lit up the room with his warmth and personality. He would be working on Angela that afternoon.

Angela only needed the one tooth pulled. Her teeth (what's left of them) are pearly white once more. While under anesthesia they discovered some small growths on the back of her tongue which seem benign and we are going to monitor (they offered me the option of biopsying, but I declined). Sally told me that the tooth was so bad that even while Angela was under sedation her body flinched when they touched it. She had been in tons of pain and kept it all to herself. This situation was dire. Animals hide their pain as a defense mechanism because the sick and the weak get picked off in the wild. Sally called me about the growths while Angela was still under. The office called in the afternoon to tell me how she was doing post-op. I not only had a relaxing afternoon, I had a good one. Angela was in good hands. And I put her there.

Sally and her office kept in touch with me the entire weekend, following Angela's progress. Angela came through with flying colors. She looked at me like she did when I was first on the phone with Sally discussing the estimate. With deep love in her eyes, she purred loudly and rubbed me with her fluffy face over and over and over again. She thanked me all weekend. There was no mistaking it. Two weeks later she's over it. We still love each other, but the fireworks are gone. She was giving me a clear message at the time. Yes. Do it. Yes. Go here. Yes. Thank you.

I got the message.

The bill came in well under the estimate and I have six months to pay it off with no interest thanks to the Kitty Kat Kredit Kard (officially called Care Credit, and I highly recommend it. There are no fees). Need I say more about Dr. Sally Haddock and her beautiful staff at the St. Marks Veterinary Hospital in New York City? It is a happy place. It is a good place.

My mom succumbed to pancreatic cancer a month before I graduated from college. She hung on for two years—eighteen months longer than the most optimistic prognosis—the fierceness of a lioness, driving her through sickness until I had made it, finally, on my own two feet. I stand in her light.

CHAPTER 22

I REMEMBER MAMA

January 24, 2012

For a long time she was absent from my life. The vacancy was epitomized by a fiery cavern in my heart, a bleeding, gaping, weeping wound.

My mother died just as my peers were starting out in life. I was supposed to be starting out, too. It was a month before my college graduation when she shed her mortal coil. Kids and their families were celebrating their accomplishments en masse, planning their lives, their moves, jobs, relationships, and futures. I organized her cremation while she was dying of cancer in the room next to me in my sister's apartment. Everything I knew and loved was ending. My life came to a screeching halt.

I was alone the day of my graduation. All my friends were with their families. I had no one to celebrate with. My only sister went on a business trip that week, and she neither gave me a graduation gift nor even took me out to dinner. She just went away, saying "You don't mind if I go, do you? You didn't really want to go to graduation, anyway, right? Isn't that what you said?" If you could ask such a question then, no, I don't need you. And no, I didn't particularly feel like participating in a mass celebration with thousands of strangers when the person I loved most in the world had just died after a long illness, and when my only "consolation" was being with a person as emotionally absent as my sister. The enormity of the festivities at my esteemed university couldn't have rubbed in any more how alone and distraught I was. Thousands of people milled about in celebration while I agonized. It poured torrential rain. The sky was black and I reflected that darkness. I was raining, too. My face and chest were soaked by precipitation cascading from clouds on my face, blurring my eyes so that I could barely see through the downpour I was generating. The water and my emotions were one. I was dizzy with despair. No one could tell. And no one cared. People were too busy running under their umbrellas, laughing, smiling, screaming and hugging. Too busy planning and celebrating. I continued to rain for years.

I lurked around my pretty college town that day, dressed up for I don't know what since I didn't go to any ceremony. Not the big one in the morning, not the smaller one at my dorm in the afternoon where people received their diplomas. My dorm house masters, a very sweet older couple, knew of my distress and my decision not to attend. They mailed my diploma to me in a cardboard tube.

I wore the dress I wore to my high school graduation and a new white denim Esprit jacket I bought myself as a graduation gift. I took myself out to lunch. There was a girl from my dorm with her dad at the restaurant. I didn't want them to see me. I ate quickly and left. I didn't want anybody to see me.

Mom had worked so hard to get me here. She'd missed out on her own college graduation because she had to drop out of school to support her parents when her dad got cancer. I went to a very prestigious school and my mother lived vicariously through me. The ivy mystique epitomized college for her. It was like a Hollywood movie set. Perfection. Excellence. All I experienced was anxiety, depression, and perma-sadness since she was dying for the last two of my four years. I worked hard. I performed in comedies and musicals and put on a stoic face. Some people actually thought I was funny, cheerful, and happy. They forgot I'm an actress. And strong. I forged huge walls and buttresses to keep myself from falling down. Or getting close to anybody. I felt alone, like *The French Lieutenant's Woman* in her hooded cape, and I plodded along. Mom's impending demise was always the prize at my finish line.

Mom pushed me to work hard and be the best, always. She was a relentless taskmaster, to me and to herself. I've since learned how important and healing it is to choose gentleness over the perpetual crack of a whip. She paid the ultimate price for her fighting attitude toward life. I believe it contributed to her cancer and her death. But it softened her, too, by the end. It took the fight right out of her. The cancer won and she could finally let go. I think it was almost a relief to her, a widow with two girls, after pushing so hard for so many years. Life was a battlefield of sorts to her. I felt closer to her in the last six months of her life than I ever had. She was in massive pain, but she was nice. No more criticizing and nit-picking. She didn't have to be vigilant anymore.

Few people understood the depths of my despair. In fact, not everyone thinks that losing a parent is so bad. I can't tell you how sick I was of hearing, "Well, *nothing's* worse than losing a child."

Fuck them, I thought, stabbed through the heart by those words. They assume a parent's pain is the only one that's really *deep* and actually *matters*. How does anyone know I didn't love my mother *more* than someone else loves their kid? Is this a competition? There was *no* pain worse than this loss in my life, the second of my beloved parents to go, and I'm not submitting my suffering for comparison and review.

If an old man's only company is his goldfish, and he loves and talks to it, when that goldfish dies, that's the worst thing that could happen to him. How dare anyone judge that as insignificant because it's "just" a fish and an old man? Anyone ever see *Harry and Tonto* with Art Carney, about an old man and his cat? I rest my case. There are parents who do not mourn when their children die. There are parents who never parented. There are parents who kill their progeny.

Some say, "It's not the natural order of things! Children are not supposed to die before their parents!"

What natural order? Do we follow a template? Are we clones with prescribed, cookie-cutter lives? Children die before their parents all the time. Children are born sick and deformed. People, both young and old, plain old die. We're assigned no guarantee or warranty when we arrive. There is no "supposed to" in this world. There is only what is. And what we do with it.

Though I believed in life after death, I was now two for two losing my parents. Dad died when I was five, Mom when I was 22. Three of my four grandparents were dead, and my fourth was in a nursing home. My belief in my parents' etheric survival was no comfort. They were gone. I told a therapist I was sad because "I don't have parents."

He argued, "Yes, you do."

Oh, that was a *real* shot in the arm. I never claimed spontaneous generation in a petri dish. If I *have* parents, Dr. Compassion, how exactly do I cash in on our connection? What an idiot. I didn't go back to him. I remained lost in my vortex of despair. Grief was the backdrop for my existence.

My healing came through spiritual seeking. I received channeled readings from the friend of a neighbor, one apartment away. My neighbor was a mess herself, in her forties, overweight, depressed, neurotic, but she was good to me. We shared a belief in the spirit world. When her friend Lynda came up from North Carolina looking like nothing so much as Pippi Longstocking at forty-five, complete with freckles, red hair in pigtails, and a gap between her front teeth, my life was changed. Lynda was in New York to shop her new psychic novel around. She was also a channel for a spirit called Milarepa. I'd never heard of Milarepa. I'd never heard of channeling.

Channeling is when someone goes into a deep meditative state or trance and brings in high-level spiritual energies. This is not the same as being psychic or mediumistic when any level of information (or spirit) can theoretically come through. The purpose of a channeled session is to educate humanity (or an individual human) on a profound level, not to predict. It's Sermon on the Mount time, not "should I date this guy?" Typically the same entity or entities will come through a particular channel. If you ask a personal question you will inevitably get a provocative answer that leads you back to yourself and your ability to choose, learn and empower yourself.

Lynn, Lynda, and I sat on Lynn's bedroom floor with a tape recorder for my first session. Lynda breathed deeply, closed her eyes, meditated and slowly toned ten to twenty om's. Her "stilling" practice took five to fifteen minutes. This country hick, complete with twang, who lived on a farm and had no money, became someone very different. A soft energy came through and its voice was hard to hear at times. Milarepa was a Tibetan poet and saint. Uh huh. I didn't care. All I was interested in was what he had to say.

His words were poetic. Careful. Amazingly, this being knew me inside and out. Lynda didn't know me at all, and Lynn didn't know me *that* well. She certainly didn't know the intricacies regarding my past, my parents, and my soul. Milarepa knew it all.

Milarepa was gentle, loving and patient with me when I was obtuse. He gave me meditations to do and prayers to say. He said it was time to let go of my mother. What was he talking about? Let go of what? She was gone. I missed my mommy. I sought comfort and he told me to stop. It was crushing.

"You should now let the entity that you knew as your mother rest, for she at this juncture is weary and has some sorting out to do. That later in your ribbon of lives, your reel of lives, like the movie screen pictures, you will once again encounter your mother and this time the roles will be switched. She has much to learn from your high shining light, and already has benefitted greatly from your beacon. But certain troubles that predated you were laid heavily at your doorstep, so to speak. You had made the decision to help in this regard, prior to joining her in this particular life frame and you were not asked to bear a burden greater than the strength of your shoulders could hoist. However, sleep is now at hand. Know that you did shine your ever bright and lovely beacon and let the weary rest. Let your *own* heart rest."

"You told me I must release my mother. I'm not sure in what ways I'm still attached. So what do I release?"

"Imagine that there is a subtle but strong connection of many tendrils. Imagine the physical visualization of two beings connected by many subtle but strengthy tendrils. Imagine that a flow of many intense emotions have been passed through these root-like tendrils. Imagine now, friend Valerie, in your mind that one by one the tendrils do become smaller, smaller, smaller until they are like the breadth of minute threads. Can you with me now visualize this? Close your eyes now and feel a sweet, soft, fragrant, wafting wind blowing away gently those thread-small tendrils. Can you feel this? Imagine now that the soft fragrant wind filled with pink flower petals does softly blow away, one by one, each thread. And so they melt from you like the spider webs in the sun. Can you feel that with me? Imagine that you now do float up a few feet into this flower petal wind, feeling my love embracing and sustaining you. Can you feel that with me? Now I want you to repeat this prayer: *'I do release, most gently, most naturally, the thread-small tendrils that in the past once connected me with my mother. I forgive her. I forgive myself. I do now release her to the wind and wish her well.'*"

Well, this depressed the fuck out of me. My love for her was being reduced to dust and detritus. As if she wasn't gone enough, he wanted me to diminish my attachment to the straws I was grasping at. It wasn't possible. I felt betrayed. He invited me to be reassured by his love. Who was he? Some dead Tibetan peace and love guy? I didn't know him. I wanted my Mommy, not some meditating saint with his hair in a bun. My attachment to her remained strong. And, apparently, dangerous.

I had really bad hives that started after my mother's death and lasted for decades. It was obviously stress related. No doctor, no antihistamine, whether topical or internal, helped me. I scratched so much my entire body was bloodied and swollen. During another session I asked, "How can I eliminate the itching of my skin, how can I lessen anxiety, negativity, and hatred of my body? How can I improve my health, both mental and physical?"

"Dear, Dear, Friend Valerie, You are not truly ailing but feeling a fierceness in the skin, in the sensory perceptors most strictly represented by the bodily touch, for it is the vessel of your skin-enclosed being. The physical Valerie, the sensory Valerie is registering this dismay of the very skin that seeks to surround her and detain her from a heavenly escape. This is a tricky time for you. The sadness in the soul, the discomfort of the body, the hatred of the body all are related, and the minute itchings do now signal to you the onset of the spring season, the time of rebirth in a Valerie-season that still seeks the solitude and cold, still comfort of the winter. But you may step into the sunshine now, Child. You must, for your time on Earth is not nearly done, though you wish to sleep and collect the still comfort you believe of the little death, a respite from the world-weary ravages that you perceive mean physical life.

"You must now begin to see that this is a fragile time of your life, for without the insight and understanding of the physical signals you could begin to sorely manifest a more serious malady. The ragged itchings, the niggling discomforts are but a timid tapping, a whispered warning. I say to you now—heed it. Do not be in love with the death state, for your wish to be with your mother is like the mourning of a lost dog for his departed master, like a lover mourning a premature death of his beloved, and these feelings of deep loss place you on a dangerous precipice, flirting, unconsciously considering, the leap.

"I must tell you now Dear, Friend Valerie, that this loss does have a power now to suck from you the vital life force. I must say to you now, Friend Child, that you are currently in a danger zone, that on the borderline of your consciousness you do demean your skin-enclosed self and do wish to forego the physical for a time.

"I say to you at this juncture that deep inside the bosom of you there is a Force. This Force is a million-fold more strong than the negative, fainting part of you that does now seek to deceive you of its power. The Bright Valerie-Force, the Life-Seeker, the Smiling Friend in your mirror is many times more strong than the negative mother-self, the temptress that bids you to sleep and shuck your bodily form. The Bright Goddess Self, the Shining Valerie Force needs now your help, needs now your faith, for I implore you once again to get in touch with her in your mirror. She is your Friend. She means you highly well. She may be seen in the shining pupil of your eye. She may be seen in the reflection on the waters of your Eye-Soul.

"Look lovingly and long into this beautiful Soul-Eye. Proceed into the sunlight. Find trees. Derive from them strength. Do not be afraid of the Life these Sap High Friends now with you share. Touch tendrils of new grass and rejoice. Say to yourself these words: '*I am the Power Valerie. Life is my lover. I embrace it. I welcome the sunshine on my skin. My skin is lovely and sun-warmed. My bones are strong and erect. My face is the visage of the Divine Goddess. I love myself as I love God's world. My purpose is Life. I happily give forth My Life Force to the abiding Earth. And Earth gives it freely back to me.*'

"You may face the death date with a feeling that you have the right to dwell on Earth, happily, and with a freedom of motion, never frozen and afraid of the returning warmth. Yes, meditate. Do so in the sun. Call to me in your prayers. I will abide with you and I will comfort you. Adieu."

Do you understand what a channeled reading is now? How no garden-variety psychic could give you something that deep? There are many compassionate and wise psychics and mediums, but true spiritual channeling is the Voice of God. She comes in many forms, and there are many, many wonderful channelers today. As we continue to grow as humans and merge with our Soul Selves, we will all be channeling all the time, speaking from and thinking with our Hearts, even when we order breakfast.

Milarepa started out all casual in this reading but then that warning kicked in, telling me that I was passively suicidal and in grave danger of tumbling into greater sickness and irretrievable darkness. It made me even sadder to realize how sad I was.

Years later I am much happier and greatly healed. This is a testament to the beauty of the myriad spiritual teachings I have sought, and the hard, hard work I've done seeking joy once more. I know now that I am a Spiritual Rock Star, Diva, Queen, Empress, Goddess of Love, Wine and Chocolate, Sex, Meditation, Tap Dancing, and Whimsy. I am Sovereign. Not raining, but Reigning now. Long Live Me.

CHAPTER 23

CHATTING WITH THE DEAD

January 28, 2012

So, boo hoo, my life was big, many sad, for big, many years, having lost my parents at an early age. I *believed* in their existence beyond the physical, but belief (which means "to give life/lief to") is not the same as *knowing*. You need tangible experience to feel something in your bones. You can't just read about surgery if you want to become a surgeon.

I was lonely. Depressed. Anxious. Sad. Angry. You name it, I wallowed in it. I know for a fact that the tortured relationships (the torture was all mine, I assure you) I had with distant, detached, self-involved men were an outcropping of the pain I felt. When you're miserable, it's not possible to attract really happy people or experiences. Like attracts like. The world always acts as our mirror. However, the torment I experienced with each relationship served me as I unleashed volatile, toxic emotions that had been kept locked inside for too long. The entanglements (and the associated release) were vehicles of healing for me though they were painful, like having a gangrenous leg amputated on the battlefield.

I've learned to trust everything in my life. That doesn't mean I *accept* (or even like) everything that comes my way. But I use discernment and set boundaries. When I choose to be with someone, or choose to be a certain way (even miserable) I own it. I chose those "off" relationships. I am no victim. And if you can accept (or consider) that, karmically, we choose *everything* in our lives, even the crappy stuff, no, *especially* the crappy stuff, you'll be moving toward healing and empowerment. Unless we are four years old, we don't go to school to learn finger painting, do we? We run tough courses when we want to challenge ourselves. Pearls are spun because of the irritation caused by grains of sand in the oyster's core. Work with the irritation in your life, bless it even, learn the lesson, accept the gift, and spin your Pearl. Behold your Beauty.

Over the course of decades I had sought healing via channeled messages. Diane, a dear friend, bought me psychic readings on my birthdays. My overweening "forever" desire was to be with my life partner and Diane understood this, along with my need to communicate with my dead parents. On some level I've been searching for my mate since losing Daddy when I was five. I get this. And yet I've never chosen a relationship in which I was nurtured, loved, supported, and safe, as I was with my father.

Milarepa (channeled spirit) told me that while I know what true love is, having had it with my parents, it is scary to me because I associate it with loss. Bingo. Sure. So I bid low and as a result my half-assed dating choices only incurred more hurt. I was afraid of the Great Wizard of Oz, but was still on the Yellow Brick Road. I associated love with longing. The carrot always dangled in *front* of me. I never allowed myself the satisfaction of feeling loved, and safe for fear of losing it all over again.

I see now, as an older, wiser and much happier person, how the path of pain has led me back to myself. How each tormented relationship helped me to excavate my past, unearth the sadness, grief, and despair that I'd evolved since my father's death when I was five and was never able to express since I was so busy tending to my mother and *her* grief. I'm a very empathetic person but the one person I was not empathetic toward was me. I sucked it up and soldiered on. Step by step, I've built a new me through introspection and hard, personal work. I've invested in my happiness. But as important as all the emotional tussling in the trenches has been to my evolution, so has the direct contact with my parents that I eventually experienced via mediums.

Years ago I went to a psychic in Red Bank, New Jersey, courtesy of my friend Diane. This medium could feel my mother's presence. That was great, cause I sure as heck couldn't.

"You're her little air (Aquarius) baby. I feel such deep love."

I started tearing up. She felt my father's energy, and said it was very different from my mother's.

She said, "They want to prove to you that they're here." This is what noted medium James Van Praagh calls "survival evidence mediumship," information that only the deceased could know, and only you can verify. Saying, "I feel such deep love" rang true but is neither specific nor verifiable.

She said, "Your mother says you had a funny dog." This was ridiculously wrong since I had no dog, funny or not (which was a real sore point from my childhood). She continued, "And you hurt your right leg when you were younger. Your parents are offering this as proof that it's *really* them." I shook my head. This was wrong, too. I broke my right *arm*, but there was no leg injury. She wasn't proving anything to me except that she was bubbly and animated.

As with many accurate readings (for I did feel this woman was connected to Spirit) this does not mean that every word of it is accurate even if some or most of it is. The two meanings did not become clear to me until later, as is often the case with psychic messages. Sara was correct on both counts, the dog *and* the leg. My sophomore year of college I twisted my *ankle* while being hazed for a humor organization. I was wearing sneakers and my rubber sole screeched and stuck on the linoleum at an ice cream parlor. I was charged by my tormentors with hopping on one leg and shouting, "Ha ha ha ha ha!" in the crowded shop. (Yes, totally embarrassing). As I started to topple I broke my fall with the objects directly in my trajectory, a man's buttocks. I desperately grabbed both of them. Imagine his surprise as he waited for his cone at the counter. My humiliation was complete.

I had to go to the hospital. My ankle was terribly swollen and I needed crutches. So when the medium said "leg" it didn't register because to me the event was "ankle." However this injury is undoubtedly what they were referring to. It was a serious wound and the pain in my foot and ankle lingered for years.

I hurt my left knee badly about four years ago in a serious bike accident. Someone chided me because I wasn't wearing a helmet.

"Well what the hell difference would it have made, my *head* was fine!" I retorted.

I had just lost my job and health insurance and was trying to figure out whether I needed to continue my Cobra payments to get further treatment (i.e., surgery). E.R. X-rays showed no breaks, but there's lots of stuff in the knee that can be seriously compromised, like cartilage, ligaments and tendons. There's complicated wiring in that joint. The attending E.R. doc was so drop dead gorgeous that time slowed as if in a movie when he approached. A friend had joined me in the waiting area and our jaws dropped simultaneously. He wrote on my discharge papers "abrasion of the skin." Hilarious. My knee was the size of a cantaloupe. I couldn't walk. The hospital put me in a wheelchair and gave me a cane. Skinned knee my ass. Cute but dumb (or just couldn't be bothered).

I prefer alternative healers to regular docs and I asked my chiropractor, Dr. Zev, whether he thought my knee would get better or need surgery. He referred me back to myself (which made me love him even more). I felt I was getting better and that I would rather treat this naturally and not worry about surgery.

He asked me, "Have you ever had a serious sprain before?"

I thought about it then remembered the ankle.

"How long did the pain last?" he asked.

I froze as I recalled the details of the injury. "Ten years." I had wondered at the time whether my ankle would continue to hurt my entire life. Eventually, I noticed the pain was gone after a full decade of twinges and discomfort. (Lately, I've been feeling it again, after 30 years!) I discontinued Cobra (that pricey snake!) and proceeded with my medical intuitive, chiropractor, and acupuncturist, which cost considerably less than the monthly mafia extortion bill and helped me heal naturally.

I had another big "a-ha" moment when I figured out what my mom was talking about regarding the "funny dog." When I was quite small I had a white, fuzz-covered, battery-operated mechanical dog. It had a collar and a leash and I took it with me on the sidewalk. It hopped slooowwly, so crossing the street was a rather treacherous undertaking, but doggie and me made it across with my mother's supervision.

The "heavenly contact" with my folks still felt ephemeral, wispy at best. Yes, it was pleasant. I believed this medium was the real deal, and I could *sense* what she was saying about my mom and dad. But I was seeking more concrete contact. That's why I studied with noted medium James Van Praagh. I had seen him on TV and found him to be remarkable. He is. He has a stunning gift. When he gave messages from the other side, the bereaved broke down with recognition and gratitude. The messages offered the possibility of healing by *proving* that our loved ones *really are here*. They still think. They still feel. They see us. They love us. They do their own healing and growing when they get to the other side. They are simply on a different wavelength. You need 3-D glasses to see them, a stethoscope to hear them. We don't question that the heart beats just because we don't normally hear it without an amplifier. Daily meditation and prayer facilitates the process of connection with Spirit, including with our own guides and teachers on the other side. If we're texting all day and listening to hip-hop, there's less of a chance that they'll get through.

My first class with James was at the Omega Institute in Rhinebeck, NY. It's a great, New-Agey joint where you can take everything from watercolor painting to remote viewing. They've got it all. Plus it's on a wooded, magical campus. It was a large group and we did exercise after exercise with James. I kept hoping he would stop the class and say, "Wait! There are two people here who absolutely *must* talk to their daughter!"

It never happened.

We did transmogrification (staring at a partner in pitch dark and watching their etheric form shift), worked with pendulums, and read each other's energy fields. I learned a lot.

At the end of the weekend class James said, "How many people were hoping to get a reading from me?" There were a good hundred fifty people in the room. At least half of us raised our hands. "And *what's* the title of this class? 'Developing Your Intuition'. *Your* intuition!" he sassed. He then proceeded to give two hours of emotional readings. I did not get a message.

Shortly after my bike accident (which was shortly after I lost my job and health insurance) I started ramping up my spirit activities. I'd been to my first séance the previous October. During this séance, I went into a light trance and received intriguing messages from two mediums (which I've detailed in other chapters). I was so impressed by the messages that when the man who gave me one said, "You should come back. Phyllis and I are running the next séance." I jumped at the opportunity. The two mediums out of a huge group who had messages for me were running the next meet? You betcha I'm going. I couldn't wait.

I was starting to feel a real, tangible connection with spirit. I returned with my cousin Genia (her dad Pete was my mom's brother). I was really hoping she would get a message. She didn't. I didn't either. At the very end of the circle her dad and brother came through. Then my mom arrived. The whole gang was there.

The medium said dramatically to me, "Your mother and her mother are *swirling* around you, *caressing* your cheeks and saying how lovely you are!"

The "swirling and caressing" took me aback, since my mother did little "swirling" in physical life. I was more used to her criticisms. The teenaged smartass in me came back to life, recreating the dynamics of our relationship.

I responded silently, "Oh yeah? I'm lovely *now*, huh? How 'bout all the times you called me *fat?!*"

The medium continued. "Change is coming!" she asserted. "Your mother says that change is coming! A new relationship is starting next month. Are you in a relationship now?"

"That would be a resilient, resounding, resplendent and thudding *no*."

She continued, "In February and March you will be creatively rewarded. What do you do?"

She was relieved to discover that I was both single and creative because it indicated that she was receiving accurately. What Mom didn't mention via the medium was "creatively rewarded" in February or March of which *year*. They're not so specific about time on the other side. Maybe they don't have watches. (I must fill you in now and let you know that the contract for my first book, the very book you are holding, was signed in early March, three years and four months after this prediction.)

Also following this prediction, I met a man the very next month. Someone unlike anyone I've ever dated, someone unlike anyone I've ever *wanted* to date. Lo! He was not a depressed, angry, obnoxious, immature, narcissistic artist. He was nice. Pleasant. Clean. Affable. I was not swept off my feet, though he cuts a very dashing figure, but I spent hours talking with him. Or rather, at him. I didn't let the poor fellow get a word in edgewise since he was the first guy who ever listened to me. There were no sparks that night, but as the evening wore on I found myself increasingly attracted as I grew aware of his compassionate qualities. I liked how he talked about people. No disdain, no bitterness, and he expressed gentle concern about one of his good friends.

Those sparks I've had in the past? Warning signs. Danger, karma ahead! Yet I needed each and every one of those experiences to learn and grow, so I have not one regret. Meeting and spending time with this man was a peaceful experience. I was accustomed to angst, longing, drama, and pain. Now I know "sparks" = "fire" = "smoke" = "burn" = "ouch." I'm tired of ouch.

I was incredibly comfortable with this man from the minute I met him. Within a few days, I realized all the prophetic signs I'd been collecting over the decades regarding "Him" strongly indicated "him," the fellow I had just met. This is the guy I've been waiting for all my life but the spirits had encouraged me to forget about since I had much to do and experience before we met.

"I cannot divulge the place and time when this relationship will occur," taunted Milarepa.

I thought they were being coy, but now I understand why. I would have slit my wrists had I known true love was coming this late in life. I wanted to get married at 18 (to who, I don't know). Now I'm looking at a wedding that may well be sponsored by AARP.

"The relationship you seek stretches out a bit further..." intoned Orkie.

The spirits have some sense of humor. My game is already in overtime and I'm still waiting for the other team to arrive.

When the relationship did not commence immediately, I became restless. I was already old in my mind when I met him, so once I figured out he was "the one" I was like, "Chop chop! Let's get going! There's no time to waste!"

But the relationship did not proceed. I became desperate for psychic information. I was convinced I was right. Ten years prior to meeting him I dreamt about *exactly* how we met, in almost photographic detail. I can still recall that dream like it was yesterday.

One of my dreams had him coming up to me, asking if I was single, which I had to think about before happily affirming, "Yes!"

He quietly and seductively said, "Finally."

Then he walked away. What? But he came back later in the dream, with a vengeance (I will not go into the torrid details). This dream was prophetic. We met. He walked away. I'm still waiting for him to come back.

I went to more séances. It was now March. I got a message from my grandmother saying I needed to go to school. School? I've been done with school ever since…going to school, so what the hell was she talking about? I concluded that the medium was off her rocker. Humoring her, I asked the medium what *kind* of school my grandmother intended since the whole premise seemed absurd. "I don't know but she was very insistent, 'Go to school! Go to school!'"

I'm skeptical about most of the messages I receive, and with good reason. You don't want to take anything at face value before you've assessed the source and whether or not the message resonates with you. Never give your discernment away, your common sense, or your power to someone else just because they have visions, even if they're accurate visions. We all receive our own messages; whether or not we pay attention to them is another story. Our dreams communicate with us. Sometimes we'll have a "feeling" (this is our gut, talking to us). Some people hear (clairaudient), others see (clairvoyant), and some know/feel (clairsentience). Always run other people's messages by your own censor. There's *no* better expert on you than *you*. We must trust our selves, our abilities, and our intuition, and stop constantly looking outside for pills, experts, and consolation via consultation. The Kingdom of Heaven is Within. When you find it inside, all gifts will then reflect it outside. The movie projector is internal. Life is the movie screen on which our thoughts and feelings manifest.

I took a nap the day after the séance and woke up knowing *exactly* what my grandmother meant. I was so excited, I cannot tell you. That medium was *not* a kook. My intuition had worked out the problem, and/or I communed with Nana while I was napping. I don't remember the dream or conversation. I just knew that "school" meant the two different psychic development classes that I was genuinely interested in taking but didn't feel I could afford since losing my job. I fought with myself but my cousin Genia encouraged me to take them.

I said, "It's counterintuitive when my income has disappeared!"

"No," she said, "It's *totally* intuitive. You have to do it."

She and my grandmother were exactly right. Dipping into savings to make them happen, those courses deepened my connection to the spirit world and my own intuitive abilities. The second one changed my life.

I went back to Omega for a second class with James Van Praagh, this time not for a weekend but a full five days. There were one hundred forty people in the group. I gave up hope that I'd get a spirit message from James, but it dawned on me that I was with one hundred forty white witches from whom I might. The class was filled with working mediums and psychics. I didn't think I was mediumistic or even particularly psychic. This class started to change my mind. We had an afternoon off (which pissed me off since I thought I'd paid for five full days). James encouraged us to form practice "development circles," and said if we were serious about developing our intuition we should "sit" or "hold circle" every week. He attended a circle for something like twenty-seven years, and he was already born powerfully psychic. Concert pianists practice every day. Psychic skills need to be developed and maintained like any other muscle.

I wanted my money's worth so I organized a practice group, pronto. We met in our gorgeous classroom with huge windows surrounded by trees and a field. There were about eight or ten of us gals (as you can imagine, the class was predominantly women, with a few exceptions). We decided to focus on one person, with one medium doing the reading. I volunteered to be read. I wrote my mother's name (Nina) on a piece of paper, folded it, and clutched it in my lap. A Russian medium sat across from me and concentrated. She was a court translator during the day, from Polish and Russian to English and back again. At night, as a medium, she translated from living to dead. I loved it. She closed her eyes and spoke with her thick accent.

"I'm getting letter M as in Mary."

Well, close, but no cigar. I thought maybe she was picking up M as in *Mom*, or M as in *Mother*, and M is awfully close to N (maybe her psychic Russian hearing wasn't so good?) but I didn't want to give it to her. You don't want to "feed" the medium with answers or leads. So I fed the medium. "Try letter N as in *Nancy*." She saw an image of me with blonde hair, red lips and nails. This was a cartoon character I played in a musical comedy right after my divorce. It seems my mother saw the show from the other side, which amazed me. I trust she had good seats. But that was all the Russian gal got.

Another woman in the circle came up and whispered in my ear, "Is it Nina?" I looked at her amazed and nodded. I didn't know any of these women, really, maybe a first name or two, but there was no intimate knowledge about me by either medium. This woman ran with the reading. I felt bad for the Russian gal because she'd been usurped. It turned out she was in awe of the reading I was about to receive, one that was about to change my life.

The medium kept her eyes closed. "Oh, I feel terrible. I'm weak, I'm *so* weak. And I'm in pain, ow! OW! Oh, my stomach…my blood is bad, oh, oh, and it's a *mess*! What a mess…"

She sat uncomfortably with all this, since unfortunately she physically experiences what she's picking up. She didn't name my mom's disease, but she very specifically and accurately described my mother's symptoms toward the very end.

"Are you aware your mother was speaking with people on the other side when she was near the end?"

"Uh, no. She was babbling incoherently."

Her body was riddled with the toxicity generated by pancreatic cancer, not to mention the morphine and other drugs I administered to help alleviate her discomfort. They didn't seem to work. She was in massive pain.

"Do you have a sister?"

"Yes."

"Older?"
"Yes."
"Is she sensitive?"
"Yes"
"A diva?
"Yes."
"Oh my God, what a pain in the ass!"
"Yes."

I was so relieved to hear my mother acknowledge the difficulties I'd had with my sister since when she was alive Mom tried to make the best of both of us. But things had changed.

The medium then proceeded to speak the name of the special man I'd met six months before. She said it three times. Loudly. Clearly. I was dumbstruck. My mother had told me at the séance with my cousin that a relationship was going to start. I met the man right on schedule, but the relationship did not commence. So, when were the games going to begin? She said no more on the topic so I let it go. I was in awe of the fact that my mother was speaking so clearly through this woman. Mom was here! The hair was standing up on my arms.

Mom communicated via the medium so naturally, so casually, that I felt as if I was having a "live" (forgive me) conversation with the dead. I felt our old, easy connection, like I was having lunch with her in real-time. Once the communication ball got rolling I felt like Helen Keller must have when she started understanding Annie Sullivan's sign language messages…Mom and I were talking! We were back in the groove. This medium conveyed her personality, vocabulary, her cultural milieu, and energy perfectly. I was electrified.

She said, "Your mother is an excellent communicator."

Of course she is! (The apple doesn't fall far from the tree.) Mom was very intelligent, an English major, and a lot of fun.

"She's pointing to the ground saying, 'When I died you were down here. Now you are up here.'" The medium's eyes still closed, she lifted her hand high in the air to indicate the healing strides I'd made. "She wishes she could have done the same for herself."

I got choked up. Ever since getting sick my mom had only become nicer. I was so used to her nitpicking and criticizing me. I know she was doing the best she could at the time based on her beliefs. We all do. I also know that learning, healing and productivity continues on the other side. We don't lose who we are. Energy cannot be created or destroyed. It's physics. We are energy. Consciousness is energy. We simply *transform*. We shapeshift into our Light Body. We lose nothing. We gain everything.

The message regarding my progress gave me insight that I wasn't just a poor, sad little orphan. And that my mom wasn't overly critical and disapproving anymore. I was this kind of cool woman whom my mother was complimenting. She acknowledged my growth. Which means she was watching me. Which means that she's connected to me, tangibly, in real-time. Here. Now. Which means I'm *not* alone. Nothing has brought me closer to *experiencing* my belief in my parents' non-physical existence than the live demo via mediumistic contact.

"Your mother has all your dead cats," the medium continued.

"*What?*" I choked.

My mother wouldn't even let me get a *hamster* when she was alive. I didn't believe it until the medium accurately described all my dead cats. My mom is saddled with them for all eternity (or until she incarnates again). Talk about karma! I think it's hilarious. That's what she gets for not letting me have a dog, cat, or hamster when I was growing up. Now she's coated in heavenly cat hair and taking out the etheric kitty litter, metaphorically speaking.

"Now she's showing me a tray of brownies. Did she bake brownies for you?"

No, she didn't. This was the first miss. Then as the memories started flooding back, it hit me like a ton of bricks. My mother was *reminding me of things I'd forgotten.* I used to make brownies for *her!* Well, actually, they were for me, the chocoholic in the family, but that was the conceit, that they were for "her." My mom was more a lemon meringue pie/baklava gal, but who has the time to make those? When my mom went to PTA meetings at night (when I was in the fourth and fifth grades) I figured out how easy it was to bake brownies from scratch using the recipe on the Baker's chocolate box. The house smelled delicious when she returned at 10 p.m. We had a sweet little party when she came home.

As wonderful and amazing as all these details were I was dying to know more about the MAN whose name my mom said *three times*. I trepidatiously asked if she had anything more to say about him. The medium repeated my question to her out loud, then repeated my mother's answer, "Hasta la vista," she said.

I felt punched in the stomach. I railed against the obvious meaning, "goodbye." Why speak his name three times if he wasn't relevant? Why tell me I'm going to meet him right before I meet him *if he's of no consequence?* It was inconceivable.

The medium said, "Is this someone you need to say goodbye to?"

"*No!*" I said vehemently. *Hell* to the no! How do you say goodbye to someone who is not there?

"Your mother is showing me the magician's trick where he pulls the tablecloth out from under a fancy place setting."

I responded, "Accurate."

I was totally on my mother's wavelength and understood the charade-like images and symbols she was communicating to me via the medium. I interpreted my mother's intentions at lightning speed. This man's entrance into my life was foretold accurately, down to the month. I met him on cue, the carrot was dangled, then unceremoniously yanked away. Man, but no relationship. The metaphor was perfect for how frustrated I felt. The rug had been pulled out from underneath me. I had the eggs, milk, butter, flour and sugar, but no cake.

"She's showing me a puppy chasing its tail."

"Accurate," I replied.

While I had just got a puppy a month ago I knew she wasn't referring to that. My mother always told me, "Don't chase *them*. Let them chase you." Ha. I was never much of a "Rules" girl. I kept reaching out to him, just simple emails, and initially he responded. It was friendly, but it didn't progress. I kept trying to engage him without pushing. I certainly couldn't let him know what I believed. Talk about a kiss of death, "But you're my *husband*!" I was alone in this. I was the puppy chasing its tail. It was humiliating. I stopped emailing.

Then my mother switched gears and rolled fast-forward. "You need to be patient. He's not going to get it at first. But when he does, it's going to move like gangbusters" Gangbusters is a word right out of my mother's lexicon. The medium laughed, "Now your mother is singing, 'I'm Gonna Wash that Man Right Out of My Hair.' Is there someone else you need to get rid of, first?"

"Apparently so." I replied.

It was only eight months since I'd been with the famous old man and he was still in my thoughts. "Okay, point taken."

"She's showing me King Kong now. Do you understand this?"

"No, I don't."

"She's showing me Tarzan, does *this* make sense?"

"None."

I still haven't quite figured those two images out yet. We loved old movies, my mom and I, but not *King Kong* and *Tarzan*.

My friends think I'm crazy for believing that this relationship will come to fruition after all this time. I don't believe in him. I believe in me. I trust my dreams, my feelings, my gut, my intuition. I received a highly accurate description of him from a psychic a full year before I met him. I trust the myriad messages from other people, many of them strangers, that point to him, even though they have variously described him as a blonde and a brunette. Those are details. I cleave to the heart of the message, what the messages have in *common*, not the minutiae that is off. If a group of psychics had him simultaneously in the next room they would each describe him variously. It's the game of "Telephone." And for those of you who don't already know, "hasta la vista" means "see you later."

Most important, my mom came back to me. I can feel her now, and I know from another psychic that she's the one knocking around my kitchen (the cabinets pop open by themselves). One psychic feels she sits at the foot of my bed at night. This is a lovely image, and it sits well with me. The "other world" is right here. It's not "up there" or "down there." It's in our midst. Just like our bodies are made up of cells and microbes we cannot see and the air is filled with microwaves, x-rays and cell phone signals we do not feel. We know them by their works. They are there. You have to align with their frequency and turn on your psychic receiver.

If one is to learn the subtle workings of spirit one must become subtle oneself. I feel connected to my mother now. I know she saw me vacuuming this morning when feathers were flying in my bedroom (my ancient down blanket finally exploded). It was a scene right out of *The Sound of Music* when Maria plays with the children or *Fanny and Alexander* (one of my favorite films) when the nanny has a pillow fight with her young charges late on Christmas night. Magic. And a mess.

Feathers can symbolize Angels. I highly recommend Lorna Byrne's book *Angels in My Hair*, if you want to get a hands-on understanding of how prayer and communion with Spirit works. It's complex. It's mysterious. It's stunning. Lorna has been seeing and communicating with angels since she was a child. Most people thought she was a moron. Read the book and decide for yourself.

Whereas in the past I missed my mother, now I love my mother. It's in real-time, and it makes a huge difference. My friend Bill invited me last minute last night to see *Wit* on Broadway, starring Cynthia Nixon. I wasn't particularly in the mood to see a play about a woman dying of cancer, even for free. Bill's mom died of cancer when he was young, like mine. I had writing to do and I was exhausted, having been up til 2 a.m. the previous night, way later than my usual bedtime.

Here's how I made my decision. I was doing the laundry yesterday (and I'll be doing it again today with all those feathers in my duvet cover, and frankly, everywhere else). My building's laundry room is in the basement and I pass by the superintendent's office to get there. The office was empty, but the TV was on and there was a bald, skinny woman with no makeup wearing a baseball cap on the screen. I identified Cynthia Nixon and knew the character's look from *Wit* because I tried to watch the HBO version but didn't like it. I haven't had TV in three years, and I don't read the paper. I didn't know there was a revival of the show on Broadway starring Cynthia. But a "flash" came to me, "Oh, she's doing *Wit*." Thirty minutes later my pal Bill invited me to the show. This is synchronicity, and I know enough now to take the hint and follow The Yellow Brick Road. Spirit gave me a preview of the evening on my super's TV.

I rallied my energies, painted my face (even though I suspected I'd cry it all off) and met Bill. The play is ninety minutes, no intermission. I remained unmoved for the first sixty minutes. *Wit* is about a very smart, very proud academic who is humbled and broken from pain, being a patient, and facing her own death. Her doctors are academic and cold, like herself. She's a John Donne scholar (*Death, Be Not Proud*) and deals with cancer via her intellect.

As she degenerates, the only thing that matters is the compassion she receives from her primary care nurse, someone she deems "not too bright." Her pride disappears as fear and vulnerability come to the fore. An old academic friend comes to visit at the end and there are sweet moments of nurturing and of humor. The tears were pouring down my face by now, but I shrieked a loud gasp of a laugh when the children's bedtime story being read to

Vivian (the patient) was peppered by amusing commentary by her friend.

When you hold back your sorrow you hold back your capacity to feel joy as well. I let them both rip—laughing and crying blend into each other now, different sides of the same coin. I know deep joy because I allowed my innards to be excavated by deep pain, my hardness softened by sorrow. The pitfall to avoid is to not let your wounds become thickened with scar tissue. Keep your heart bravely open. The bombs, both "soft" and "hard" that explode and devastate only make your heart cavity Bigger. Keep it Big.

I'll close with an end quote from the movie *Kama Sutra*, where love and loss are inextricably tied:

"Knowing Love
I will allow all things to come and go
To be as supple as the wind
And take everything that comes with great courage
"My heart is as open as the sky."

AFTERWORD

Dear Readers, one of my editors asked, "What about the guy? What about *the guy*?!" As we go to press, he still has not manifested. (The dreams, signs, and messages regarding him continue unabated, as does my faith.) However, you will be the first to know when he does.

Are you kidding me? It'll be the greatest story ever told! I'm excited to tell it, and even more excited to live it.

I would like to acknowledge medium Jennifer Hicks, for she is the one who brought my parents back to me in living color and gave many of the laser beam readings referenced in this book. You haven't even heard my father's otherworldly confessions. It's beyond big. The mystery he initially presented through Jennifer is still slowly unraveling.

Hello to my mate/husband/male-counterpart, wherever (and whenever) you are.

About the Author

Valerie Gilbert is an actress, solo-performance artist, and story teller now translating her ability to make others, laugh, cry, and sit on the edge of their seat into a writing career. Born into an ardent metaphysical family, she is passionate about exploring the depths and heights of the Divine Mystical Human Experience. She shares this enthusiasm with others via her writing and the weekly meditation and psychic development group she leads.

An avid environmental, animal and peace activist, Gilbert is a native New Yorker, Harvard graduate, and member of the Dramatist's Guild. She lives in New York City with her muses Angela (cat) and Mimi (dog) and looks forward to marrying the man she's been dreaming about for ten plus years. Author photo by Paolo Bonaccorsi.

www.ingramcontent.com/pod-product-compliance
Lightning Source LLC
Chambersburg PA
CBHW052017070526
44584CB00016B/1794